I owe this bool
Amos Alonzo Stagg and

In appreciation of the support
College Football Hall of Fame —
came up with the idea to do this
be donated to the C

For more information about t
available for purchase, visit the
website: ww

Books by Don Gwaltney

The Steak Lover's Handbook
Characters, Legends and $3 Bills
The Bandit Joaquin, An Orphaned Mexican's Search for Revenge in the California Gold Rush
The Not to be Forgotten Forties
The Best Pizza Recipes in America
Knollwood: How One of the World's Great Golf Clubs Came to Be.
Legends of the Heisman

Copyright © 2000 by Apple Core Press, 11 Ibis Lane, Spring Island, South Carolina 29910

First printing 2000

Library of Congress Cataloging-in-Publication Data:
Gwaltney, Don

Library of Congress Catalog Card Number: 00 134455
International Standard Book Number: 0-9639591-6-6

Design and production by Connie Miley Cook

Photo production by Stuart Cook

Proofed and edited by John Gwaltney

Printed in the United States of America by TMS Incorporated, Racine, WI

APPLE CORE PRESS
11 Ibis Lane
Spring Island, SC 29910

ATTENTION CORPORATIONS, UNIVERSITIES, COLLEGES AND PROFESSIONAL ORGANIZATIONS: Quantity discounts are available on bulk purchases of this book for educational (or training) purposes (or fund raising). Special books or book excerpts can also be created to fit specific needs. For information, please contact the Fulfillment & Distribution Department at Apple Core Press (address above). Or, call 843-987-9451.

LEGENDS OF THE
HEISMAN

by Don Gwaltney

Heffelfinger, Carideo, Nagurski, Rentner, Crowley, Stagg, Warburton, Munn, Oosterbaan, Dodd, Oliphant

Clarence Munn was an All America guard for Minnesota in 1931. He was a giant, so big his college nickname stuck: from then on, he was known as Biggie. Years later, Biggie Munn coached Michigan State to the '52 national championship.

and a few dozen others were men who performed mighty deeds across the nation's gridirons on long ago autumn Saturday afternoons by making comeback catches, last second tackles and game breaking gallops. By so doing they not only popularized the game but immortalized themselves. The Sunday morning papers have long since frayed and yellowed but the headline makers shall shine forever. The first part of this book on the Legends of the Heisman is dedicated to the deeds of these men, a tribute to the men who made the game a significant part of life in America seasons before the Heisman trophy was awarded.

What college football was like before the Heisman and the hype

Some folks, mostly easterners, would have you think that college football, like most everything else, was something invented out east and performed out there until only recently.

Well, the first part of that is right. Football did begin out east. But like most things of worth, it didn't take very long for the western folk to catch on to it and then get very good at it – even go somewhat beyond. Case in point: Not too many teams have recently switched to the East Coast Offense.

An artist's rendition shows Princeton and Rutgers competing in the first college football game ever played in 1869. The men from Rutgers won the initial meeting 6-4.

Football started on a cold day in the east when someone (history has forgotten) suggested a modification of the game of Rugby, pitting a team of 25 men against an opponent of like number.

The team of 25 along with a few faithful followers boarded a train in Princeton for New Brunswick. There, starting at 3 o'clock on November 6, 1869, after a leisurely dinner, some billiards and some girl-watching, Rutgers and Princeton played the first game of intercollegiate football.

Accurate accounts of this game have been impossible to come by. The accepted source is from the Rutgers Targum, the student paper, and it speaks of "grim men, silently stripping" before the kickoff. What they stripped to isn't revealed, but it wasn't much even though the day was so cold there was a serious threat of snow in the air.

The players simply took off their hats, coats and vests and they were ready. No uniforms. The only color was provided by scarlet turbans the Rutgers boys wore on their heads.

The scoring of that game, patterned after Rugby, was six goals for Rutgers, four for Princeton. Princeton won the return match in a shutout, eight goals to zero and the game of football was launched. The Princeton schedule was one game with Rutgers in '70, a couple of games with seminaries in '71 and one game with Rutgers in '72. The '73 season saw Princeton put a three-game win streak against the Yale Bulldogs. Princeton won and won seven more times before finally losing to Yale in '76. The '77 Yale-Princeton game was 0-0.

By '81, Princeton was playing a 9-game schedule. In addition to Yale and Rutgers, teams from Pennsylvania, Columbia, Harvard and even far-west Michigan were on the list. North Carolina and the Carlisle Indians were added in '99, Notre Dame in '23 and Ohio State in '27. The Tigers never did make it out to the west coast, though Yale did in '99 (that's 1999, against University of San Diego).

By the time the game of football was 20 years old, it already had the makings of widespread popularity – included in its repertoire were heroes, uniforms, nicknames, rivalries and records. One of the former was

above: Yale vs. Princeton, 1890
*right: **Knowlton "Snake" Ames '90**, holds the Princeton career touchdown record (62) and was one of the first-ever consensus All Americans.*

Knowlton "Snake" Ames of the Princeton class of '90. Snake was not only drop-dead handsome, he also more than measured up to his memorable monicker. Snake and Yale's Amos Alonzo Stagg were the ends on the first consensus All America team, tallied at the end of the '89 season.

Snake wasn't the only one with a nickname. Thirteen years earlier, his Princeton predecessors showed up for the annual Yale game with an orange P on their jerseys and four years later they added orange stripes and, according to one scribe, "played like tigers." Now, 124 years later, they're still officially known as the Tigers.

A major Tiger feat in the 80s was a 65-yard field goal by James Hexall in yet another loss to Yale.

By '90, the service teams were involved. Navy beat Army 24-0 in front of a couple thousand officers, ladies of the post and assorted Navy Midshipmen – about 102,000 short of how many nowadays watch one of the most colorful rivalries in college football.

Joining Snake Ames on the early edition of the Princeton All America list were Hector Cowan '88, Roscoe Channing '90 and Edgar Allan Poe '91. And for the records, please note that in '93 the Princeton Tigers whomped the Yale Bulldogs 6-0 in New York City in front of 40,000, ending Yale's 37-game win streak and winning for the Tigers the national championship.

The U.S. Naval Academy started playing football in 1879. This is one of its earliest teams. In due time, Navy made both its Midshipmen and its footballers more presentable for the camera.

Amos Alonzo Stagg, Pudge Heffelfinger and/or Albie Booth would have won the Heisman.

It was a factor of timing. The reason none of the above Yalies won the hallowed Heisman was because they were born too soon. Stagg and Heffelfinger played some 47 years before the first Heisman; Booth three years ahead of it.

For sure they were good enough. Stagg and Heffelfinger were bona fide legends on the most dominating team ever. The combined score of their 1888 team against 13 opponents was 684 to 0.

Heffelfinger grew up in Minneapolis and learned the game in high school by playing with the University of Minnesota varsity. By the time he got to Yale, he was of monstrous proportions for the times. The 6-3, 210-pounder was also swift and agile. He was the original pulling guard – the first guard to pull out and lead interference.

As a freshman, Heffelfinger single-handedly wrecked the Princeton flying wedge. When it got started, he came at it full bore and then went airborne. He drew his knees up and hit the startled apex man squarely in the chest. Later, when the apex man went into a crouch, he dove over his head and landed on top of the ball carrier. He became a college coach but continued to play the game until late in life. At age 48 he scrimmaged against the Yale varsity and injured two players before being asked to leave. He continued to play football until his 66th birthday.

Pudge Heffelfinger, Yale guard and three-time All American from 1889 to '91, was part of the '88 Yale team that ran up 684 points while shutting out all 13 opponents.

Hey, that's all true. And Amos Alonzo Stagg was just as incredible. He was born in the middle of the Civil War, in 1862. Due to a lack of funds, he waited until he was in his late twenties to go to college. At Yale, he pulled double duty. He was a player-coach. When he was 27, he and teammate Pudge were named to the first All America football team. That was in '89.

Two years later, a fellow named James Naismith called Stagg and invited him to participate in a game he was in the process of inventing: basketball.

Stagg played in that first game and for that contribution is in the Basketball Hall of Fame as a player (he's also in the Football Hall of Fame twice – as a player and as a coach).

Before the turn of the century, Stagg was head coach at the University of Chicago and won a western championship with the Maroons. He won his first national championship with them in '05.

Twenty-seven years later, Stagg was still coaching the Maroons. One of the players he recruited, Jay Berwanger, won the first Heisman. By then Stagg had been known as the Grand Old Man of Football for some time. He was 70 years old but far from through coaching. When the University of Chicago retired him, Stagg relocated to tiny College of Pacific in Stockton, California.

It took a few seasons for Stagg to develop a winning program at Pacific. In '43, a year dominated by service football teams, his Pacific team went 7-2-0 and was ranked 19th in the nation. The venerable coach was given a rare tribute by peers that included such coaching legends and Paul Brown, Lynn "Pappy" Waldorf, Bernie Bierman, Frank Leahy, Red Blaik, Fritz Crisler and Bennie Oosterbaan. For that year, they voted the 81-year-old Stagg the NCAA Coach of the Year.

Stagg still wasn't through. In '46, when he was 84, he was one of the best recruiters in the country. He put together a squad good enough to set an NCAA scoring record by the time they were seniors. That was the '49 Pacific team that went undefeated. It was ranked 10th in the country and Stagg was on staff as an assistant coach. The team was led by Stagg recruit Eddie LeBaron, who finished sixth in the Heisman that year and then went on to quarterback the Washington Redskins.

After putting Pacific in the big time, Stagg signed on as an assistant at nearby Stockton Junior College and continued to coach until 1960. He retired at age 98 and died at 102. His contributions to the game were numerous. No less than Knute Rockne said of him: "All football comes from Stagg."

Albie Booth was also an amazing man. He stood just 5-7 and weighed only 144 pounds. But on the gridiron, he was a giant. Saturday after Saturday, great throngs packed the Yale Bowl, titillated by the prospect of what Albie was going to do. Had he been surrounded by supporting personnel similar to those fielded at Notre Dame, Booth would have accomplished the steady headlines of Red Grange or Jim Thorpe.

Booth was a '32 graduate of Yale. That was three years before the first Heisman trophy was awarded. In his Eli career, Booth rushed for 1,428 yards. He also intercepted eight passes and returned 76 kicks for 1,138 more yards. He scored 17 touchdowns, converted 24 extra points and kicked four field goals for a total of 138 points.

*After starring at Yale and then coaching football for 38 years, **Amos Alonzo Stagg** earned the title of the Grand Old Man of Football. That's what they called him here in 1930, as he addressed a new squad of footballers (the University of Chicago) for the 39th time in his career. But Mr. Stagg was far from through. This was a ritual Mr. Stagg would repeat 30 more times.*

Mighty Michigan

fielded its first football team in 1879, beating Racine 1-0 in front of 500 and playing Toronto to a 0-0 tie in front of 2,000. Three years later, the Wolverines journeyed to the Ivy League for three games in five days and lost to Harvard, Yale and Princeton. That did it for a while. Michigan played no games in '82 and then went 2-3 in '83, losing to Yale 46-0 on Nov. 21 and to Harvard by 3-0 the following day. Michigan did master the game before the century was over and between 1901 and '05 compiled a 56-game unbeaten streak which included a 49-0 thrashing of Stanford in the first Rose Bowl on 1-1-02. In that game, the playing field was 110 yards long, both touchdowns and field goals counted for five points, a team had to make five yards in three downs and forward passes were not allowed.

right: **Southern California's first football team: 1888.** *Note the early west coast influence on the game. When Rutgers and Princeton started the game, they had 25 players per side. The USC version required less than half that number.*

Michigan made its debut in college football in 1879. *Right after the turn of the century, the Wolverines would field the best team in the country.*

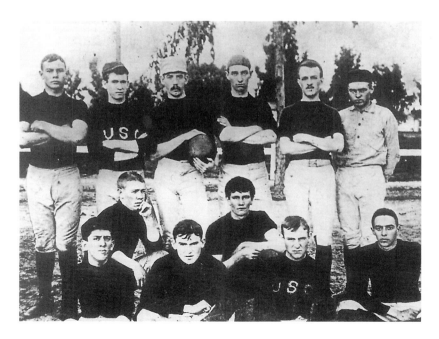

By the turn of the century, football was big time out west.

Princeton University's 1893 Varsity football team featured three future Michigan head coaches: William McCauley, WIlliam Ward and Langdon "Biff" Lea.

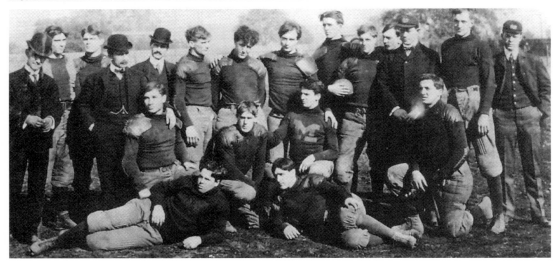

Michigan's 1901 squad. On ground, left to right: Willie Heston, Arthur Redner. Middle Row: Ebin WIlson, Herb Graver, Harrison Weeks, unidentified. Standing: unidentified, Everett Sweeney, Bruce Shorts, Keene Fitzpatrick (Trainer), Charles Baird (Director of Athletics), A.E. Herrnstein, George Gregory, Dan McGugin, unidentified, Hugh White (Captain), Curtis Redden, Fielding H. Yost (Head Coach), Neil Snow, Crafts (Manager).

Boola Boola! *This Yale fight song was first sung on Saturday, Nov. 24, 1900 at the Yale-Harvard game.*

The 1908 Tigers *were the biggest Tiger team in LSU history, averaging 180 pounds a man. They were undefeated, untied and nearly unscored on. They won all 10 of their games by lopsided scores. They beat Texas A&M 26-0, Mississippi State 50-0, Baylor 89-0, Louisiana Tech 22-0 and Arkansas 36-4.*

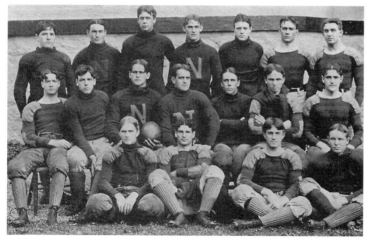

The 1898 Navy Midshipmen *finished 7-1, but they did not play Army that year.*

Now it was Paul Robeson's turn to show violence. After several failed attempts at beating him, the white boys started glancing at Coach Sanford, wondering how long the mismatch carnage would last.

When Paul Robeson walked onto the practice field for the first time in 1915, he was not greeted warmly by the men he hoped to call teammates. He probably didn't know it then, but at that time he was but one of three black men who had come this close to playing college football.

One was Fritz Pollard at Brown, who along with the janitor was one of two black men on campus. There was also a guy at Harvard and now Paul Robeson, the son of a runaway slave who had become a minister in highly segregated Princeton.

The coach was George Foster Sanford. His introduction to Rutgers football technique was to run play after play at the newcomer to see how he could stand up.

Robeson recalled it like this. "They ran the first couple of plays right at me. After the third one, I was stretched out

Paul Robeson,
Rutgers end. Inside that uniform was one hell of a man.

on the ground with my hand extended palm up. A player stepped on it. I thought it was broken but it wasn't. But a couple of fingernails came off."

He got up and took his position. Now it was Paul Robeson's turn to show violence. After several failed attempts at beating him, the white boys started glancing nervously over at Coach Sanford, wondering how long the mismatch carnage would last. Finally, the coach cupped his hands around his mouth and hollered across the field, "Robey, you just made the varsity."

He was tremendous. On offense, he played end and was occasionally moved to the backfield to run with the ball. But mostly he served as the point blocker, coming at the defense from as many as seven different positions, shredding the opposition and opening enormous holes. On defense he played the equivalent of today's middle linebacker and was a devastating tackler. He also kicked off, kicked extra points and called the plays.

He played four years for Coach Sanford, starting 31 games. The record was 22-6-3, with Rutgers scoring 941 points to 191 for the opposition. He was awesome on both sides of the ball at blocking, catching, intercepting and dismantling.

He was a two-time All American. He was also elected to Phi Beta Kappa and was valedictorian of the class of '19. He won the college oratorical contest four straight years and gave the commencement address. He won 12 letters in four sports. Then he played three years of pro ball, to earn money for law school at Columbia.

He was a giant in many ways. He stood 6-3 and weighed 215. He became an actor, singer and lecturer. He was on Broadway and in the movies. He made his signature song "Ol Man River" a classic. He was also a victim of the hearing room of the House Un-American Committee and never were the words of a man of such deep integrity and courage so manipulated.

It took time for the truth of Paul Robeson to come to light. He died in '76. Appreciation was yet to come, but come it did. In '88 he was named to the Rutgers Sports Hall of Fame. Rutgers has also named three buildings for him. Finally, in 1995, he was elected to the College Football Hall of Fame.

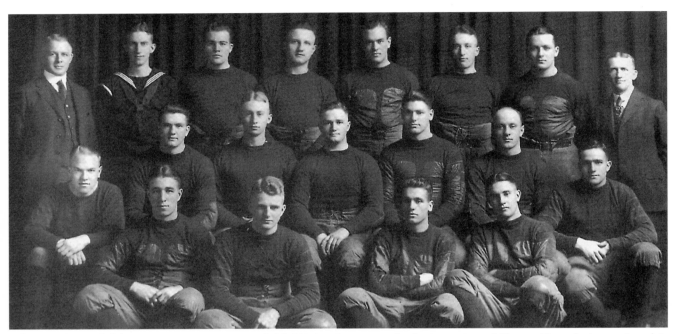

The 1918 Michigan team *was one of 11 Wolverine squads that captured the national championship. Between 1918 and '33, Michigan was football's most dominating team, with four national titles and a record of 97-21-7.*

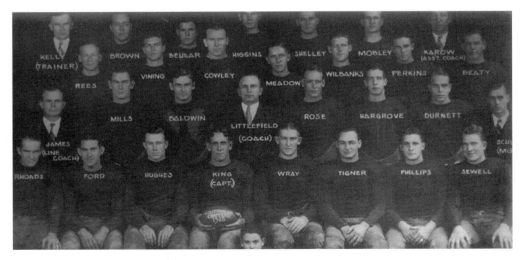

The 1928 Texas Longhorns *won five of six conference games to claim Texas' fourth SWC crown.*

In the early twenties, the Buckeyes made their move.

While Michigan was establishing itself as a national power, the boys from Ohio were coming on strong. In '19, Ohio State outscored its opponents 176-12 for a 6-1 record and its first-win ever over Michigan, 13-3. The next year was even better. OSU went unbeaten and took a 7-0 record to the Rose Bowl. Unfortunately, Buckeyes got clobbered out in Pasadena by California 28-0, but this did not diminish soaring interest in OSU football. In '20, the Buckeyes started an extensive campaign to build a new stadium and over a million dollars was pledged by proud and dedicated Ohio State fans.

Ohio State followed the great '20 season with a 5-2 record in '21 and its third consecutive win over mighty Michigan. The stage was now set to make it four in a row over Michigan in the brand new stadium. Those who had cited concerns that the new Ohio Stadium would be too large looked on in awe as the stadium was officially dedicated prior to the Michigan game on October 21. Temporary stands were erected in the south end of the stadium and a crowd of 72,500 (pictured above) was estimated.

The new stadium was a huge success. The local football team was not. Michigan was on its way to a 6-0-1 and conference-championship season with a scoring edge of 183 to 13. The Wolverines spoiled the stadium's dedication by shutting out the Buckeyes 19-0.

The eyes of the N.Y. Downtown Athletic Club would have been on these players, too.

Christian "Red" Cagle joined the Army backfield in 1926 and became the first Cadet to win All American honors three times.

Brice Taylor, Southern California guard and the Trojans' first All American, was 10 years ahead of the Heisman. It would also be 36 years before an African American would win the Heisman.

Ted Petoskey was an All American end on the 1932 Michigan national champ team. He helped Michigan win three conference titles and also lettered in baseball and basketball.

The 1924 Army team lost once, by a 31-7 decision to Notre

Dame, a game in which sportswriter Grantland Rice made Notre Dame's veteran backfield of Don Miller, Elmer Layden, Jim Crowley and Henry Stuhldreher famous. He penned one of the most colorful sports leads ever written: "Outlined against a blue-gray October sky, the Four Horsemen rode again. In dramatic lore they are known as Famine, Pestilence, Destruction and Death. These are only aliases. Their real names are Stuhldreher, Miller, Crowley and Layden."

The Four Horsemen, HB
Don Miller, FB
Elmer Layden, HB
Jim Crowley, QB
Harry Stuhldreher

1927 All Americans

ENDS
BENNIE OOSTERBAAN,
Michigan
TOM NASH, Georgia

TACKLES
JESSE HIBBS, USC
BUD SPRAGUE, Army

GUARDS
BILL WEBSTER, Yale
JOHN P. SMITH, Notre Dame

CENTER
LARRY BETTENCOURT,
St. Mary's

BACKS
CHRIS CAGLE, Army
GIBBY WELCH, Pittsburgh
BRUCE CALDWELL, Yale
HERB JOESTING, Minnesota
BILL SPEARS, Vanderbilt

Elmer Oliphant, Army halfback,
1915-17

Bennie Oosterbaan, 1925-27, the Michigan end who caught most of Friedman's passes, was a three-time All American. He was also All American in basketball and All Big 10 in baseball. After playing, Bennie returned to his alma mater to coach Michigan to three Big 10 titles and a national championship while earning coach of the year honors in '48. He stayed on as Michigan's coach for 10 more seasons.

T. F. "Puny" Wilson, *Texas A&M Halfack, 1922*

Jack Buckler, *Army halfback, 1932*

Bronko Nagurski. Which came first, the player or the name?

When one is given a name like Bronko at birth, one is expected to grow into massive manhood, be possessed of Bunyanesque power and play adult games as if all the other fellows were still in diapers. Do you think Mike Ditka's mother intended for him to be a hairdresser? Did anybody at Chicago Vocational High School prophesize that Dick Butkus would design wedding cakes? Can you imagine a flight attendant named Steve Stonebreaker? Or a florist named Leo Nomellini? If you owned a department store and wanted someone to do your windows, would you call on the likes of Bulldog Turner, Bruno Banducci, Gino Marchetti, John David Crow, Jack Pardee, Sonny Sixkiller, Cliff Battles, Elmer Angsman, Choo Choo Justice, Pistol Pete Pihos, Hurryin Hugh McElhenny, Bucko Kilroy, Chuck Bednarik, Joltin Joe Perry, Mac Speedie and Night Train Lane? Highly unlikely.

A few men were placed on this

planet to be football players. When Bronko Nagurski first appeared on that there farm up in Rainy River, Canada, he was destined to be a Minnesota Golden Gopher and not just a Chicago Bear but the original Monster of the Midway.

By the time Bronko grew up, there was no limp in his wrist nor anywhere else on his hulk. He was only a couple inches over six feet and weighed but 226 pounds. But he was rock solid and strong as a grown bull in a pasture full of heifers. He had a 19-inch neck, huge arms and hands and powerful shoulders. When he carried the ball it took four to bring him down. Two would grab hold of him, another would try to knock him off balance and another would try to finish him off.

Hey, am I exaggerating? Here's what an opponent said about Bronko: "See these lumps on my head? I got most of them trying to stop Nagurski." That came from Steve Owen, former New York Giant. Owen went on to say, "There's only way to defense him. Shoot him before he leaves the locker room. He is the only back I ever saw who ran his own interference."

As you would expect, Nagurski was an All American at Minnesota. At two positions. Tackle and fullback. He didn't just turn pro, he helped establish pro football. George Halas saw all the great football players in his day. Many of them played for Halas. None surpassed Nagurski. He would have racked up awesome rushing numbers for the Bears but rushing was only one of the jobs Halas assigned him. On offense, Bronko was usually a blocker for the the herd of thoroughbred backs on the Bear roster. On the

occasion when Bronko got the ball, not much could stop him. You've probably heard the one about the time the Bears needed a touch from down on the two-yard line on fourth down and they gave it to the big guy. Bronko didn't stop at the goal line. He slammed into the ivy at Wrigley Field. You know what's behind that ivy? Brick. It didn't hurt Bronko.

Folks don't usually recall this about Bronko. He could pass. He won the pro championship for Halas in a '32 playoff game against Portsmouth by throwing a game-winning TD to Red Grange. Can you imagine those two in the same backfield? A year later, in the first official NFL championship game, he threw for two TDs in a victory over New York.

Nagurski played for Halas from '30 to '37 and then abruptly left when Halas wouldn't pay him what he asked for. When Halas went into the service in the early forties, Bronko came back and helped the Bears win the '43 championship. He got a TD in the win over Washington for the title.

I remember going to a dinner for Vince Lombardi at the Chicago Athletic Club back in the sixties. Every great name in midwest football was on the dais. Halas, Lombardi, Luckman, Christman, Angsman, Hornung, Lattner, Lujack and a bunch of others were introduced to applause. They saved Bronko for last. He didn't stand. He just raised one finger, one on which he wore one of his championship rings. It would have been a bracelet on anybody else. Everybody in the room stood up to clap.

1928 All Americans

ENDS
IRV PHILLIPS, California
JOE DONCHESS, Pittsburgh

TACKLES
JESSE HIBBS, USC
OTTO POMMERENING,
   Michigan
FRANK SPEER, Georgia Tech

GUARDS
SERAPHIM POST, Stanford
RUSS CRANE, Illinois

CENTER
PETER PUND, Georgia Tech

BACKS
CHRIS CAGLE, Army
KEN STRONG, NYU
DUTCH CLARK,
   Colorado College
HOWARD HARPSTER,
   Carnegie Tech
CHUCK CARROLL,
   Washington

1929 All Americans

ENDS
WES FESLER, Ohio State
JOE DONCHESS, Pittsburgh
TACKLES
BRONKO NAGURSKI,
   Minnesota
ELMER SLEIGHT, Purdue

GUARDS
JACK CANNON, Notre Dame
RAY MONTGOMERY,
Pittsburgh

CENTER
BEN TICKNOR, Harvard

BACKS
CHRIS CAGLE, Army
FRANK CARIDEO, Notre Dame
RALPH WELCH, Purdue
GENE McEVER, Tennessee
ALBIE BOOTH, Yale

Mel Hein, *Washington State Center. His 1930 team was 9-0 before losing to Alabama in the Rose Bowl.*

1930 All Americans

ENDS
WES FESLER, Ohio State
FRANK BAKER, Northwestern

TACKLES
FRED SINGTON, Alabama
MILO LUBRATOVICH,
   Wisconsin
TURK EDWARDS,
   Washington State

GUARDS
BARTON (BOCHEY) KOCH,
   Baylor
TED BECKETT, California

CENTER
BEN TICKNOR, Harvard
MEL HEIN, Washington State

BACKS
FRANK CARIDEO, Notre Dame
MARCHY SCHWARTZ,
   Notre Dame
ERMY PINCKERT, USC
LEN MACALUSO, Colgate
BOBBY DODD, Tennessee

1931 All Americans

ENDS
JERRY DALRYMPLE, Tulane
VERNON (CATFISH) SMITH,
Georgia

TACKLES
JACK RILEY, Northwestern
JESSE QUATSE, Pittsburgh

GUARDS
JOHNNY BAKER, USC
BIGGIE MUNN, Minnesota
HERMAN HICKMAN,
Tennessee

CENTER
TOM YARR, Notre Dame

BACKS
MARCHY SCHWARTZ,
Notre Dame
GUS SHAVER, USC
ERNY PINCKERT, USC
BARRY WOOD, Harvard
PUG RENTNER, Northwestern
JOHNNY CAIN, Alabama

1932 All Americans

ENDS
PAUL MOSS, Purdue
JOE SKLADANY, Pittsburgh

TACKLES
ERNIE SMITH, USC
JOE KURTH, Notre Dame

GUARDS
BILL CORBUS, Stanford
MILT SUMMERFELT, Army

CENTER
PETE GRACEY, Vanderbilt

BACKS
HARRY NEWMAN, Michigan
WARREN HELLER, Pittsburgh
DON ZIMMERMAN, Tulane
JIMMY HITCHCOCK, Auburn

1933 All Americans

ENDS
PAUL GEISLER, Centenary
JOE SKLADANY, Pittsburgh
BUTCH LARSON, Minnesota

TACKLES
FRANK WISTERT, Michigan
FRED CRAWFORD, Duke
CHARLEY CEPPI, Princeton

GUARDS
BILL CORBUS, Stanford
AARON ROSENBERG, USC

CENTER
CHUCK BERNARD, Michigan

BACKS
COTTON WARBURTON, USC
BEATTIE FEATHERS, Tennessee
DUANE PURVIS, Purdue
GEORGE SAUER, Nebraska
CLIFF MONTGOMERY, Columbia
JACK BUCKLER, Army

1934 All Americans

ENDS
DON HUTSON, Alabama
BUTCH LARSON, Minnesota

TACKLES
BILL LEE, Alabama
BOB REYNOLDS, Stanford
SLADE CUTTER, Navy

GUARDS
CHUCK HARTWIG, Pittsburgh
BILL BEVAN, Minnesota

CENTER
DARRELL LESTER, TCU

BACKS
DIXIE HOWELL, Alabama
PUG LUND, Minnesota
BUZZ BORRIES, Navy
BOBBY GRAYSON, Stanford

They didn't wear mouth guards or face masks, there were no time-outs for TV commercials, they played both ways for 60 minutes and no squad had room for a specialist.

The All-Time, All-American Team, 1951

(Left to Right) Wilbur Henry, Washington and Jefferson tackle, 1915-19; Walter Eckersall, Chicago quarterback, 1902-06; Bronko Nagurski, Minnesota tackle, 1927-29; Red Grange, Illinois halfback, 1923-25; Jim Thorpe, Carlisle halfback, 1907-12; Knute Rockne, Notre Dame coach, 1914-30; Germany Schulz, Michigan center, 1907-08; Bennie Oosterbaan, Michigan end, 1925-27; (kneeling) Ernie Nevers, Stanford fullback, 1925; Pudge Heffelfinger, Yale guard, 1888-91; Don Hutson, Alabama end, 1932-34; Bob Suffridge, Tennessee guard, 1938-40.

Then, in 1935, they started the Heisman thing. And the college football hero of all time each year never had it so good.

Winning the Heisman is like going to heaven while you're still in college and you have your whole life ahead of you on earth.

They'll even make movies about you.

The John W. Heisman Memorial Trophy is presented each year by the Downtown Athletic Club of New York to the nation's outstanding football player.

Winning the Heisman has become bigger than winning the lead in a Broadway hit, a record contract, an Emmy, even an Oscar...shoot, even the lottery. The Heisman is tantamount to absolutely nothing that the world has to offer. It is, without comparison, the greatest prize every young American male with a normal load of testosterone most cherishes.

In the first place, the Heisman is awarded but once a year.

In competition for it are all the country's college football players in the prime of their lives in the best shape most will ever be in. Some 250,000 of them. Not to mention the millions of wannabes who couldn't make the squads.

And there's only one winner per year.

And as soon as he receives it, his reputation is set. His Heisman will forever be the major reason for his fame. From that day forward, he's a genuine legend.

Regardless of what each year's Heisman winner accomplishes the rest of his life – from getting named All Pro or being inducted into the College or NFL Hall of Fame or returning to his school to become its head football coach or athletic director or becoming hugely successful in business or entertainment or any endeavor whatever – the person will forever be remembered and introduced as "the guy who won the Heisman."

Ever heard of a guy named Jay Berwanger? Won the Heisman, didn't he?
Back in 1935...

First, a little Heisman history

The chaps who started this Heisman thing have long been at the leading edge of sport. They are the members of an establishment affectionately known as "The DAC," a.k.a. the Downtown Athletic Club of New York City. The members of the DAC hang out not just at a club but at a skyscraper. The DAC is a 35-story building (built in 1930) that sports a commanding view of the North River and lower harbor

and its facilities include no less than 137 hotel rooms, seven banquet rooms, a huge dining room, one of the world's finest fitness centers, a gym, an Olympic pool and assorted courts for squash, handball, racquetball, basketball and volleyball. There are 2,000 members of the DAC. Their clout is such that other athletic clubs across the country and around the globe happily admit them if they but flash a DAC card.

Back in 1935, the DAC chaps decided to display their admiration of college football by creating an annual award to the outstanding college football player in the United States. The award would be presented at the end of the '35 season.

The first order of business was to create a trophy. A committee was named and what transpired could have been an historical first: the committee came up with a good idea. The trophy would be a replica, in bronze, of a muscular footballer driving for yardage.

To create this trophy, a well-known sculptor was hired. That was Frank Eliscu, a prize winner of the National Academy. To get it right, Eliscu then hired Ed Smith, a halfback from NYU, as his model. A rough clay model was presented to the DAC committee and to make sure it would be authentic they went uptown to get a bona fide expert to pass final judgment. That person was the football coach at Fordham, Jim Crowley – the same Jim Crowley who in earlier life was one of the Four Horsemen at Notre Dame.

It appeared right to Crowley. To make doubly sure, he took it to practice and showed it to his players and had one of them, running back Warren Mulrey, take various positions on the field to illustrate and verify the sidestep, the forward drive and the strong arm thrust of the right arm. All this was done for the benefit of Mr. Eliscu, who closely observed these action sequences and modified his clay prototype to proceed. The result was a truly lifelike simulation of player action. It was then converted into a plaster cast, a step preliminary to ultimate production in bronze. And don't you know that the Heisman pose has been struck thousands of times a season by Heisman hopefuls on every gridiron in the country.

What should they call the trophy?

In 1935, it was called the DAC Trophy, presented to University of Chicago's Jay Berwanger by the Downtown Athletic Club of New York City. When word got back to DAC members that Berwanger thought so little of the DAC trophy that he loaned it to his Aunt Gussie for use as a doorstop, they decided to give it a classier and catchier name.

On October 3 in 1936, DAC Athletic Director John W. Heisman passed away, giving DAC members an excellent opportunity to rename their handsome new bronze statue: the Heisman Memorial Trophy.

John Heisman was the first athletic director of the Downtown Athletic Club. He was singularly qualified for this position by virtue of an outstanding athletic career. He played varsity football at Brown and Penn and then moved on to success and stature in coaching. His coaching career spanned 36 years, from 1892 through 1927, at such institutions as Auburn, Oberlin, Clemson, Georgia Tech, Akron, Penn, Washington & Jefferson and Rice.

Heisman was considered a gifted football coach. He was a winner and ranked right up there with the likes of Alonzo Stagg, Pop Warner, Clark Shaughnessy, Fielding Hurry-Up Yost and Knute Rockne. He was an avid student of the game and was credited with many of its innovations.

Heisman has become the most-mentioned football coach of all time. There is a constant Heisman Watch that goes on all football season long, culminated by the annual hour-long National Heisman Television Special which announces each year's winner.

1935

Jay Berwanger,
University of Chicago Halfback

He played at a school that put academics ahead of athletics, for coaches famous for molding quarterbacks. His first Chicago coach was Amos Alonzo Stagg, the inventor of the T formation. His second was Clark Shaughnessy, who perfected the split T. But Berwanger did not play quarterback. He played halfback and nearly everything else for an ordinary team in the toughest conference in the country, the Big Ten. In the three years he played, Chicago was 11-11-2. He rushed for 1,839 yards, averaging 4.19 per carry. His career total offense total was 2,760 yards, which included 50 passes for 921 yards but didn't include averaging 25.7 yards on 34 kickoff returns, punting for a 37.3 average and handling all kickoffs and extra points. He scored 152 points on 22 TDs and 20 extra points. On defense, he was a vicious tackler.

He was also Chicago's track team. At 6-1 and 195, he was the conference's best athlete. He ran the 100 in 9.9, ran the 120-yard high hurdles (15.6 seconds), the 440 (49 seconds), pole vaulted (12-6), high jumped (5-8), broad jumped (24 feet) put the shot (38 feet) and threw the javelin (190 feet). Berwanger launched not only the Heisman, but the National Football League draft. He was the first player ever drafted by the NFL. He turned it down in favor of a business career.

He made everybody's All American team in '35 and the significant All Century teams, including Sports Illustrated's. In the first Heisman voting he beat Monk Meyer of Army, William Shakespeare of Notre Dame and Pepper Constable of Princeton.

Berwanger was so unimpressed by winning the Heisman, the trophy served as his Aunt Gussie's doorstop for its first 10 years.

1935 Season Statistics:

Rush: 119   Yds: 577   TD: 6
Runners-Up: 2. Monk Meyer, Army
3. William Shakespeare,
Notre Dame
4. Pepper Constable, Princeton

1936 Larry Kelley,
Yale End

From the angle of tradition, no school has a more illustrious football history than Yale. It began in 1872, when there were 20 players on a side. The 20 Yale Bulldogs played one game that year, beating Columbia 3-0 and establishing a winning tradition unmatched by any other college. Yale has won more than 800 football games, more than any other college in America, and has outscored opponents by more than 15,000 points. Yale has produced 70 All Americans, six Rhodes Scholars and 27 men for the College Football Hall of Fame.

Yale's football influence spread across America. The Bulldogs provided more than 100 football coaches for other schools, including the first coaches at Stanford, Duke, Army, Pennsylvania, West Virginia, Dartmouth, Washington, Lehigh, Chicago, Springfield and California.

By '36, Yale had enjoyed 28 unbeaten seasons and 11 national championships. But its football greatness was now in its past. Ivy League football was waning and for several seasons Yale wasn't even dominant in that company. Yale has recently reclaimed a measure of greatness. In '99, Yale was unbeaten and untied.

The voters for the Heisman must have been much impressed by Yale's tradition when they chose their '36 recipient of the trophy. That year, on its way to a 7-1 season, Yale lost to Dartmouth 7-11 and squeaked by Princeton 26-23 and Harvard 14-13. The captain of that team was one Larry Kelley.

Not much information on Kelley was supplied by the Yale Sports Information Office. His stats weren't that impressive. It's a mystery why Mr. Kelley won the award. One explanation is that Yale football had been around for 74 years and the Heisman trophy only one. Sammy Baugh, who finished fourth, went off to the NFL to play some pro ball for the Washington Redskins.

1936 Season Statistics:
Rec: 17 Yds: 372 TD: 6
Runners-Up: 2. Sam Francis, Nebraska
3. Ray Buivid, Marquette
4. Sammy Baugh, TCU
5. Clint Frank, Yale

1937

Clint Frank,
Yale Halfback

The voting staff for the '37 Heisman must have been inundated by codgers and Ivy Leaguers. As they did in '36, they passed on a whole passel of great teams and players on the way to choosing the '37 captain from Yale, Clint Frank.

The voters had to be swayed by Yale's illustrious history. The Bulldogs had a pretty good season in '37, but it was in the Ivy League. And far better football was now being played in other parts of the country. Jack Sutherland had a powerhouse at Pittsburgh and California was rated right behind them. Fordham's Blocks of Granite forged an unbeaten season and Alabama was 9-0 and ranked only fourth. Yale was twelfth.

Clint Frank did have an impressive season, though one would be hard pressed to find out what it entailed from the current Yale Sports Information Office. Other sources, far more cooperative, confirm that the members of the Maxwell Football Club of Philadelphia also named him the most outstanding football player in the nation in '37.

Though Frank's stats weren't that overwhelming and

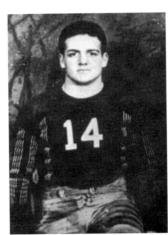

Heisman hype, even civil, mannerly cooperation with the media was yet (still, in this writer's opinion) foreign to Yale sports info hacks, young Mr. Frank did achieve a degree of notoriety. In addition to winning the Maxwell, he made the All America team in '36 and '37 and was fifth in Heisman balloting in '36. Not bad for someone lacking good stats and publicity.

Frank used the Heisman to good advantage and learned from it. He figured that if he could do this well without good publicity, he could do even better with it. So he started an ad agency in Chicago and ran it successfully for most of the rest of his life.

1937 Season Statistics:
Rush: 157   Yds: 667   TD: 11
Runners-Up: 2. Byron White, Colorado
3. Marshall Goldberg, Pittsburgh
4. Alex Wojciechowicz, Fordham
5. Joe Kilgrow, Alabama

1938

Davey O'Brien,
Texas Christian Halfback

Davey O'Brien established the Heisman as the standard of excellence in every facet of college football. At 5-foot-7 and 118 pounds, he emerged as one of the finest football players in Dallas high school history. Two years later, beefed up to 140 pounds, he took over the quarterback position at TCU from none less than Slingin' Sammy Baugh. And for the next two seasons, O'Brien was flat awesome.

O'Brien succeeded Baugh in far more than chronology. In '37, he led TCU in punting, rushing and passing. He also set the national record for the number of punt returns (58), total punt and kickoff returns in a season (72) and total punt returns in a career (116 in only two seasons). He led the country in passing in both '37 and '38. He broke all of Baugh's TCU passing records and led the Horned Frogs to the '38 national championship. His completion percentage, yards gained and touchdowns all were national records and many of his records stood for years. His TCU coach, Dutch Meyer, said of him, "He was the best play selector and greatest field general I ever saw."

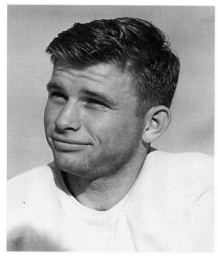

He led his Horned Frogs to a 15-7 win over No. 6 Carnegie Tech in the '39 Sugar Bowl, sealing the win with a game-saving open field tackle from his safety position. Like his predecessor Slingin' Sammy, Davey did it all. But in college, Davey did it even better.

O'Brien not only won the Heisman in '38 but also the Maxwell and Walter Camp awards. So great was his fame that he finished fourth in the AP's annual ranking of U.S. athletes, ahead of such immortals as Joe Louis, Hank Greenberg and Jimmie Foxx.

1938 Season Statistics:

Att/Comp: 194/110   Yds: 1,733   TD: 19
Runners-Up: 2. Marshall Goldberg, Pittsburgh
3. Sid Luckman, Columbia
4. Bob MacLeod, Dartmouth
5. Vic Bottari, California

1939

Nile Kinnick,
Iowa Halfback

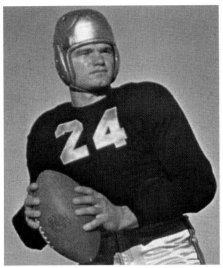

When one recalls the greatest halfbacks of all time, the name Nile Kinnick doesn't always come up. He played for Iowa in the dying days of the Great Depression and racked up unimpressive rushing numbers, averaging barely over three yards per carry and scoring but five touchdowns in '39, the year he won the Heisman. And Kinnick did not lead Iowa to the national championship. Eight teams finished ahead of Iowa in '39.

Yet when the editors of Sports Illustrated picked their All Century team, they saw fit to name Nile Kinnick to first team defense, ahead of such legends as Jim Thorpe and Johnny Lattner.

It wasn't size nor speed that made Kinnick famous. He was the smallest – at 5-foot-eight and 170 pounds – and slowest of all the Iowa backs.

As you've suspected, he was tough. Playing on a one-win-all-season team, he made All Big Ten as a sophomore. The next year, he played the entire season on a broken ankle. Again, one win. Finally, in his senior year, Kinnick put it all together. He became an expert punter and drop kicker and had outstanding success as a running and passing tailback. He beat Notre Dame 7-6 by scoring Iowa's touchdown, kicking the extra point plus 16 punts for a 45.6-yard average. With two minutes to play, he sealed the victory by punting from his own 34 and putting the ball out of bounds on the Notre Dame five. It was the upset of the decade.

Kinnick was a Phi Beta Kappa and a leader. He would have made a great senator or president. Instead, in '43 he ditched a Grumman F4F Wildcat Navy fighter plane in open seas to avoid endangering other planes on the deck of the U.S.S. Lexington. The nation mourned his death.

1939 Season Statistics:
Rush: 106   Yds: 374   TD: 5
Runners-Up: 2. Tom Harmon, Michigan
3. Paul Christman, Missouri
4. George Cafego, Tennessee
5. John Kimbrough, Texas A&M

1940 Tom Harmon,
Michigan Halfback

When Tom Harmon was a junior at Michigan, he served notice to the nation in a spectacular fashion that he was in the running for the Heisman. In the '39 game against Nile Kinnick's Iowa team, Harmon scored all the points (including a TD on a 90-yard interception return of a Kinnick pass) in a 27-7 Michigan win. That year, he joined Kinnick in the All American backfield and finished second in Heisman voting.

The next year was all Harmon's as he polished off one of the greatest college careers of all time. He led the nation in scoring for the second year in a row. In his three-year career, he ran and passed for 3,438 yards, threw 16 touchdown passes, kicked 33 extra points and a pair of field goals and scored 33 touchdowns.

Harmon's last college football game – the annual showdown with Ohio State – was one of the greatest ever played by a Wolverine (or a Buckeye or anybody else, for that matter). Harmon rushed for 139 yards and two touchdowns, completed 11 of 12 passes for

151 yards and two more touchdowns, scored four extra points, intercepted three passes (including one for a touchdown) and averaged 50 yards per punt, leading Michigan to an overwhelming 40-0 victory. In a rare tribute to a Wolverine in Columbus, the 73,000 fans all gave Harmon a standing ovation as he left the stadium.

That performance clinched the Heisman for Harmon and put his 7-1-0 Michigan team third in the national ranking, behind unbeaten Minnesota and Stanford. He also won the Maxwell Trophy, was voted MVP in the Big Ten and was named the AP Male Athlete of the Year.

1940 Season Statistics:

Rush: 191   Yds: 852   TD: 16
Runners-Up: 2. John Kimbrough, Texas A&M
3. George Franck, Minnesota
4. Frankie Albert, Stanford
5. Paul Christman, Missouri

1941

Bruce Smith,
Minnesota Halfback

When Bruce Smith was a junior at Minnesota, he served notice to the nation in a spectacular fashion that he was in the running for the Heisman. Sound familiar, like the start of the Tom Harmon chapter?

It gets even more bizarre. As Harmon did to Kinnick, so Smith did to Harmon.

The Harmon-led Michigan team would have won the national championship in '40 if it hadn't been for the Minnesota junior. In that historic game, Michigan controlled most of the play on a muddy field.

The Minnesota footballers trailed 6-0 in the last quarter when they took a touchback on a Michigan punt and had the ball on their own 20-yard line. Bernie Bierman, the wily Gopher coach, shifted Smith from left to right half, then gave him the ball on a counter play.

Smith quickly broke into the clear, needing to evade only one man – the hardnosed, speedy and soon-to-be Heismanized Tommy Harmon himself – to go all the way. This Smith did, faking Harmon into committing his

tackle too soon. Smith's run for a touchdown was 80 yards, and an extra point gave Minnesota a 7-6 triumph. The Smith-led Gophers beat Michigan for the national championship in '40 and they won it again behind Smith in '41.

Smith made a habit of salvaging victory in flashy, long-run fashion. He also scored come-from-behind touchdowns to beat Nebraska and Ohio State. And there was an Iowa game when he sat injured on the bench for the first half. In the second half he handled the ball but seven times yet accounted for every Minnesota score in a 34-13 win.

1941 Season Statistics:

Rush: 98   Yds: 480   TD: 6
Runners-Up: 2. Angelo Bertelli, Notre Dame
3. Frankie Albert, Stanford
4. Frank Sinkwich, Georgia
5. Bill Dudley, Virginia

1942

Frank Sinkwich,
Georgia Halfback

Unlike his Heisman predecessor, Frank Sinkwich did not burst into the annals of gridiron lore by faking out the current Heisman winner and dashing 80 yards for a national championship TD. No, this flat-footed, wide-butted tailback who "ran like a lady trying to get out of her girdle" toughed his way to football fame.

His legendary teammate, Charley Trippi, who later played with Paul Christman, Elmer Angsman and Pat Harder in the NFL's "Dream Backfield," said of Sinkwich, "Tough as any guy I ever played with."

Sinkwich was in the national spotlight all season long in '42. Georgia was ranked first in the country until Auburn upset the Bulldogs, 27-13. Going into the final game of the season it looked as if everything were lost. Georgia Tech hadn't lost a game and had even beaten Notre Dame in a game that brilliantly displayed the talents of a freshman named Clint Castleberry. It's a shame there was no TV those days. Sinkwich and Trippi vs. Castleberry would have generated more than a little hype.

Georgia wiped out Georgia Tech, 34-0, went on to the Rose Bowl to whitewash UCLA 9-0 and Flatfoot Frankie won the Heisman, thereby to be cradled forever in the bosom of Bulldog idolatry.

Coach Wallace Butts would say later that the team of '41 and '42 was the greatest of his time in Georgia. Sinkwich led the nation in total offense in '42 and the list of Georgia records is still freely sprinkled with his name. The record he set for total offense in a season, 2,187, still stands. And don't forget; he shared time with Trippi, the sophomore. Together, they helped Georgia rack up 4,725 yards, an SEC record.

1942 Season Statistics:
Att/Comp: 166/84   Yds: 1,392   TD: 10
Runners-Up: 2. Paul Governali, Columbia
3. Clint Castleberry, Georgia Tech
4. Mike Holovak, Boston College
5. Bill Hillenbrand, Indiana

1943 Angelo Bertelli,
Notre Dame Quarterback

When Angelo Bertelli was in high school in Springfield, Massachusetts, he was named the most valuable player in the western part of that state and nicknamed "The Springfield Rifle" for his passing ability. At the beginning of his sophomore year at Notre Dame in '41, he was running on the seventh team at halfback – until new coach Frank Leahy felt the need for a strong passing attack and "discovered" Angelo.

At that juncture in his career, Bertelli was wondering if he'd ever even get into a game at Notre Dame. He was fourth string on the freshman team. Then, over night, Leahy moved him to starting tailback. The biggest promotion in college football history was a move Leahy did not regret for a moment. By season's end, Bertelli had passed for over 1,000 yards and was second in the balloting for the Heisman.

Behind Bertelli, the Fighting Irish finished third in the country in '41. Then, because of the ability of Bertelli, Leahy switched to the T formation in '42. That year, the Irish finished sixth. And by '43, the T brought the Irish their first national championship since the era of Knute Rockne and did much to immortalize Mr. Leahy.

The scribes of the country thought so highly of Bertelli that they voted him the Heisman in '43, even though he missed the last four games. After leading the Irish to a 33-6 win over No. 3 Navy, Bertelli left Notre Dame for Marine training at Parris Island, South Carolina. And to this day, it is said of him: In all of Notre Dame's history there was no finer passer than Angelo Bertelli.

1943 Season Statistics:
Att/Comp: 36/25   Yds: 511   TD: 10
Runners-Up: 2. Bob O'Dell, Pennsylvania
3. Otto Graham, Northwestern
4. Creighton Miller, Notre Dame
5. Eddie Prokop, Georgia Tech
6. Hal Hamburg, Navy
7. Bill Daley, Michigan
8. Tony Butkovich, Purdue
9. Jim White, Notre Dame

1944 Les Horvath,
Ohio State Quarterback

At the conclusion of the '42 season Les Horvath thought he had accomplished everything possible in college football. He had played for the legendary coach, Paul Brown, and had a remarkable season, leading the Buckeyes to their first national championship. So he quit football and entered the Dental School at Ohio State.

Carroll Widdoes replaced Brown in '44 and made an unusual pact with Horvath. Discovering that Horvath had an extra year of eligibility because of wartime rules, Widdoes promised that the 23-year-old Horvath wouldn't have to practice all the time and would be flown to away games, allowing Horvath more time to study.

Horvath agreed and enjoyed a brilliant season. The layoff obviously didn't bother him, as he set a Big Ten rushing record. In addition to leading the conference in rushing (669 yards) and total offense (953 yards), he also accounted for 1,248 all-purpose yards.

The Buckeyes finished the '44 season undefeated at 9-0. The AP voted Army national champs with Ohio

State second. OSU fans claimed an unofficial "Civilian National Championship." In '44 Ohio State was the only non-service team in the top six. No less than 11 of the top 20 teams in '44 were service teams. Ohio State received an invitation to the Rose Bowl, but faculty representatives from around the Big Ten disallowed the trip.

Horvath, who played both quarterback and halfback on offense and safety on defense, was named the Big Ten's Most Valuable Player in '44. He then became the first of five Buckeyes (so far) to win the Heisman.

1944 Season Statistics:

Rush: 163   Yds: 924   TD: 12
Runners-Up: 2. Glenn Davis, Army
3. Felix Blanchard, Army
4. Don Whitmire, Navy
5. Buddy Young, Illinois

1945

Doc Blanchard,
Army Fullback

By any name, Felix "Doc" Blanchard and Glenn Davis – "Mr. Inside" and "Mr. Outside;" or "The Touchdown Twins" – made up the finest pair of running backs to ever share a college backfield. They ruled college football from '44 to '46, stealing the attention of an entire nation and leading Army to three consecutive national championships.

Many claim that Blanchard was the best prospect of those championship Army teams. He was a punishing athlete who could run, block and catch. He was a tremendous complement to the speedy Davis.

Blanchard initially attended the University of North Carolina. But after being turned down by their Navy V-12 program because they considered him overweight, he enlisted in the Army, took basic training and finally got an appointment to West Point. It was for sure the V-12's loss.

Like Davis, Blanchard was a three-time All American selection. For his career, he rushed for 1,666 yards and scored 38 touchdowns on 26 rushes, seven receptions,

four interceptions and one kickoff return.

Coach Red Blaik wrote of Blanchard: "He was the best built athlete I ever saw: 6 feet and 208 pounds at his peak, not a suspicion of fat on him, with slim waste, Atlas shoulders, colossal legs. For a big man Doc was the quickest starter I ever saw. And in the open field he ran with the niftiness of as well as the speed of a great halfback. If he had been serious about it, Blanchard could have become an Olympic decathlon star."

The Touchdown Twins combined to score 97 touchdowns and 585 points from '43 to '46, a mark that still stands as an NCAA record. More significantly, their legacy will forever stand the test of time.

1945 Season Statistics:

Rush: 101   Yds: 718   TD: 13
Runners-Up: 2. Glenn Davis, Army
　　　　　　　3. Bob Fenimore, Oklahoma A&M
　　　　　　　4. Herman Wedemeyer, St. Mary's
　　　　　　　5. Harry Gilmer, Alabama

1946

Glenn Davis,
Army Halfback

Nobody ever had a more illustrious football career than Glenn Davis. He was brilliant from the very beginning. In high school in LaVerne, California, he scored a record 256 points in his senior year. In his sophomore year at Army, he made the All America team with teammate Doc Blanchard. He led the nation in scoring with 120 points. He also averaged an amazing 11.1 yards per carry in that '43 season.

Among his honors in '43 were "Outstanding Halfback of the Year" by Walter Camp, "Outstanding Player of the Year" by the Maxwell Club and the Helms Foundation and second in Heisman voting to Les Horvath of Ohio State. The next year he again made All America, won the Helms Foundation trophy again and was once more runner-up for the Heisman, losing by a narrow margin to teammate Blanchard.

In his senior year, the three-time All American won everything. Davis finished his Army career with 2,957 yards rushing, 855 yards passing and an eye-popping total of 59 touchdowns scored (43 rushing, 14

receiving and two punt returns). His career rushing average of 8.26 yards per carry remains an NCAA record.

"Anybody who ever saw Davis carry the football must have realized that there could not have been a greater, more dangerous running back in the history of the game," wrote Army coach Red Blaik. "He was emphatically the greatest halfback I ever knew. He was not so much a dodger and side-stepper as a blazing runner who had a fourth, even fifth gear in reserve, could change directions at top speed, and fly away as if jet-propelled." (Ed. Note: Nice piece of writing, Mr. Blaik.)

1946 Season Statistics:

Rush: 123   Yds: 712   TD: 7
Runners-Up: 2. Charlie Trippi, Georgia
3. John Lujack, Notre Dame
4. Felix Blanchard, Army
5. Herman Wedemeyer, St. Mary's

1947 John Lujack,
Notre Dame Quarterback

How loaded was Notre Dame in the forties? They were often two deep in All Americans. Example: When Heisman-winner Angelo Bertelli left for the Marines in '43 with four games left on the schedule, John Lujack took over as the Irish quarterback. All Lujack did was help the Irish to three national championships and earn a reputation for himself as one of the great T-formation signal callers in college football history.

In Lujack's first start, against Army in '43, he threw for two scores, ran for another and intercepted a pass in a 26-0 victory. He played all but four minutes of those final four games. With him at quarterback, the Irish never lost. Then he went out for the basketball team and made the first team. He went out for track and won his monogram, specializing in the high jump and javelin. He went out for the baseball team and lettered in that, getting a triple and two singles in his first game.

Then Lujack took some time off from Notre Dame athletics to serve as a lieutenant in the Navy for nearly three years. When he returned he earned consensus All America honors as a junior and senior on two more Notre Dame championship teams, in '46 and '47.

No slouch as a runner (he played halfback on offense and defense as a sophomore), Lujack also punted. And he made his best single play on defense. He preserved a scoreless tie in '46 between the second-ranked Irish and top-ranked Army by making a touchdown-saving tackle of Cadet fullback Doc Blanchard from his defensive back position. He finished third in the Heisman in '46 behind Glenn Davis. Besides winning the Heisman in '47 he also won the AP's male athlete of the year award.

1947 Season Statistics:

Att/Comp: 109/61   Yds: 777   TD: 9
Runners-Up: 2. Bob Chappius, Michigan
3. Doak Walker,
        Southern Methodist
4. Charley Conerly, Mississippi
5. Harry Gilmer, Alabama
6. Bobby Lane, Texas
7. Chuck Bednarik, Pennsylvania
8. Bill Swiacki, Columbia

1948 Doak Walker,
Southern Methodist Halfback

Many of the greatest halfbacks in college football history performed in the forties and by the time the decade was over the Heisman was established as the premier award in the sport.

The players were so good then and the talent so deep, you could build a heckuva backfield from the stars who didn't win the Heisman. Stars such as Squirmin' Herman Wedemeyer of St. Mary's, Creighton Miller of Notre Dame, Buddy Young of Illinois, Georgia's Charley Trippi, Michigan's Bob Chappius and Charlie Choo Choo Justice of North Carolina came close and will forever be remembered, but they just didn't quite win the Heisman. Justice put up awesome numbers for the Tarheels but had to settle for two second-place finishes.

Another player who had to wait for his time in the limelight was SMU's great halfback, Doak Walker. He burst into national prominence as a freshman in '45, when he was named one of the first string halfbacks on the All-Southwest Conference team.

Walker then went into the service for a year. When he returned, he picked up where he left off.

He was on the All-SWC team for three consecutive

years, from '47 to '49. He also made the All America team those three years. And in his junior year, in '48, he averaged five yards a carry and led SMU to an unbeaten season and a team ranking of third in the nation. Walker finished first in the Heisman, ahead of NC's Justice.

In '49, Walker was joined in the SMU backfield by another All American, Kyle Rote. Rote was so good the SMU Heisman vote was split and Walker finished third. The following year, Rote was second.

1948 Season Statistics:

Rush: 108   Yds: 532   TD: 8
Runners-Up: 2. Charlie Choo Choo Justice,
North Carolina
3. Chuck Bednarik, Pennsylvania
4. Jackie Jensen, California
5. Stan Heath, Nevada
6. Norm Van Brocklin, Oregon
7. Emil Sitko, Notre Dame
8. Jack Mitchell, Oklahoma

1949 Leon Hart,
Notre Dame End

Charlie Choo Choo Justice racked up 5,000 yards for North Carolina and punted for a 42.6-yard average but didn't quite win the Heisman, finishing second in both 1948 and '49. In '49 he finished behind a lineman! An end who caught only 19 passes all year!

That would be Leon Hart of Notre Dame.

Just how good was this guy Hart? More to the point was how good Notre Dame was when Hart played for them. A four-time letter winner, Hart never played on the losing side during his years in a Notre Dame uniform as the Irish went 36-0-2 and claimed three national championships.

Hart gained a reputation as an outstanding blocker and superb rusher on defense in addition to his estimable pass-catching skills. With the advent of two-platoon football, he was one of the last of two-way players.

People besides the Heisman voters thought highly of him. He was a three-time first-team All American and twice a consensus choice.

In '49 he was voted the AP male athlete of the

year, outpointing such famous names as Jackie Robinson, Sam Snead and such football greats as North Carolina's Justice, Doak Walker of SMU, Arnold Galiffa of Army, Eddie LeBaron of Pacific and Clayton Tonnemaker of Minnesota.

Hart also received the Maxwell Award as top collegiate player in '49. A mechanical engineering major, he called defensive signals and often played fullback in his senior season to confuse defenses. He went on to play eight seasons with the Detroit Lions.

1949 Season Statistics:

Rec: 19   Yds: 257   TD: 5

Runners-Up: 2. Charlie Choo Choo Justice,
North Carolina
3. Doak Walker,
Southern Methodist
4. Arnold Galiffa, Army
5. Bob Williams, Notre Dame
6. Eddie LeBaron, College of Pacific
7. Clayton Tonnemaker, Minnesota
8. Emil Sitko, Notre Dame

1950 Vic Janowicz,
Ohio State Halfback

The '50 Ohio State season had its biggest victory way back in the early weeks of '48 – not on the field, but in the Registrar's office. OSU won national acclaim for winning one of the most intense recruiting wards of the decade. Vic Janowicz, a high school All American from Elyria, Ohio, turned down offers from 59 other schools and opted to stay home and play for the Buckeyes.

Three football seasons later, fans of Ohio State were not disappointed. The first game of the '50 season was a thriller, featuring Heisman winner Janowicz and runner-up Kyle Rote. Rote and SMU won that one, 32-27, but much more was to be heard from the kid from Elyria.

In the fifth game of the season, sporting a 3-1 record, the Buckeye junior led his mates to a 83-21 whomping of Iowa. In that game, he sent two kickoffs out of the end zone for touchbacks, recovered two fumbles on defense, scored on an 11-yard run, returned a punt 61 yards for a touchdown, threw a 12-yard scoring strike and kicked three extra points – all in the first five minutes of the game.

In late November, against Michigan in a driving snow storm with the wind swirling and the goal post barely visible, he booted a 38-yard field goal to win that storied "Snow Bowl." That kick was labeled one of the "Greatest Feats in American Sports" by a panel of sportswriters.

Many call Janowicz the greatest Buckeye ever. He excelled in every phase of the game – from running, blocking passing and tackling to kicking. After graduation, he played two years of baseball with the Pittsburgh Pirates, then starred at halfback for Washington in '54.

1950 Season Statistics:
Att/Comp: 77/32   Yds: 561   TD:12
Runners-Up: 2. Kyle Rote, Southern Methodist
3. Red Bagnell, Pennsylvania
4. Babe Parilli, Kentucky
5. Bobby Reynolds, Nebraska
6. Bob Williams, Notre Dame
7. Leon Heath, Oklahoma
8. Dan Foldberg, Army

1951

Dick Kazmaier,
Princeton Halfback

The significance of winning the Heisman was never more pronounced than in '51. Today, among senior football buffs across the nation, the name Kazmaier still stirs the gridiron soul – while hardly a handful can recall the name of the runner-up (answer below).

By the time Mr. Kazmaier won a starting position at Princeton, the school did have some history behind it. The Tigers started the sport, losing to Rutgers six goals to four in the very first football game back in 1869. Princeton won the return match 8-0 the following week and there have since been 28 undefeated seasons for Princeton elevens. No less than 118 players have made All American while 16 players and five coaches have made it to the National Football Hall of Fame.

Heading this stellar list of gridiron heroes is the '50-51 All American halfback who personified to Princetonians what the game was meant to be. They hand out the John P. Poe-Richard W. Kazmaier Trophy every year and this is what it takes to win it: "In addition to proving himself a player of ability, the person must

best exemplify the following traits and characteristics: loyalty and devotion to Princeton football interests, courage, manliness, self-control and modesty, perseverance and determination under discouraging conditions, observance of the rules of the game and fairness toward opponents."

In addition to establishing those exemplary standards, Mr. Kazmaier also acquitted himself quite admirably statistically, leading Princeton to 9-0 seasons in both '50 and '51. In his college career, he handled the ball 289 times for 2,404 yards (an average of 8.32 yards per attempt – an all-time Princeton record).

1951 Season Statistics:

Rush: 149   Yds: 861   TD: 9
Runners-Up: 2. Hank Lauricella, Tennessee
3. Babe Parilli, Kentucky
4. Bill McColl, Stanford
5. John Bright, Drake

1952 Billy Vessels,
Oklahoma Halfback

For several years after the Great Depression, thanks to a writer named John Steinbeck, folks from Oklahoma were known as Okies. It was a demeaning monicker until a few lads like Billy Vessels came along to bury the Okies and immortalize the Sooners.

Oklahoma first made college's big time in '46 under one-year coach Jim Tatum. Then Bud Wilkinson took over. The Sooners went from a national ranking of 16th in '47 to 5th in '48 to 2nd in '49 to No. 1 in '50, setting up the fifties as the "Decade of the Sooners."

In '52, three Sooner backs made the All America team: quarterback Eddie Crowder from Muskogee, Buck McPhail from Oklahoma City and Billy Vessels from Cleveland, Oklahoma. The center also made it: Tom Catlin from Ponca City.

As a sophomore, Vessels was the star of the '50 national champ team, scoring 15 touchdowns. But he saved his best season for last. Creating a new meaning for the word "versatile," the Cleveland slasher was part of every phase of the Sooner offensive attack. Besides rushing for 1,072 yards and a 6.4-yard average, he also connected on seven passes for 165 yards and two

touchdowns from his halfback slot in Wilkinson's feared Split T formation.

The '52 Sooners went 8-1-1, finishing fourth in the nation and winning the university's ninth conference title. OU opened with a 21-21 tie with Colorado and then reeled off four straight wins, averaging 47.1 yards a game. OU's only loss was 27-21 to No. 3 Notre Dame but the Sooners rebounded to win their last three games by a margin of 135-27.

1952 Season Statistics:

Rush: 167   Yds: 1,072   TD: 17
Runners-Up: 2. Jack Scarbath, Maryland
3. Paul Giel, Minnesota
4. Don Moomaw, UCLA
5. John Lattner, Notre Dame
6. Paul Cameron, UCLA
7. Jim Sears, Southern California
8. Don McAuliffe, Michigan State
9. Don Heinrich, Washington

1953 John Lattner,
Notre Dame Halfback

What do Paul Giel of Minnesota, Paul Cameron of UCLA, Alan Ameche of Wisconsin, J.C. Caroline of Illinois and J.D. Roberts of Oklahoma share in common? They all finished behind John Lattner in Heisman voting in '53.

Lattner claimed the trophy in the second-closest voting balloting in history despite the fact that he didn't lead the Irish in rushing, passing, receiving or scoring. A jack of all trades, he benefitted from helping Coach Frank Leahy's final Notre Dame team to a 9-0-1 record that earned the Irish a No. Two national ranking behind 10-0 Maryland.

Lattner received the Maxwell Award as the top collegiate player both as a junior and senior and finished fifth in '52 Heisman voting behind Billy Vessels, Jack Scarbath of Maryland and the player he barely beat in '53, Minnesota's Paul Giel.

A consensus All American as both a junior and senior on offense and defense, Lattner made his mark by running, catching and passing while also returning punts and kickoffs and intercepting 13 passes in his college career. He established a record for all-purpose yards that stood as an Irish record for 26 years. Yet

another example of his versatility: he gained 321 yards on only eight kickoff returns in his senior year.

Lattner played one year with the Pittsburgh Steelers before entering the service and suffering a career-ending knee injury in a military game. For several years he was a restaurant owner in Chicago, then he became an executive for a business forms company. He was elected to the National Football Foundation Hall of Fame in '79.

1953 Season Statistics:

Rush: 134   Yds: 651   TD: 6
Runners-Up:
2. *Paul Giel, Minnesota*
3. *Paul Cameron, UCLA*
4. *Bernie Faloney, Maryland*
5. *Bob Garrett, Stanford*
6. *Alan Ameche, Wisconsin*
7. *J.C. Caroline, Illinois*
8. *J.D. Roberts, Oklahoma*
9. *Lamar McHan, Arkansas*

1954

Alan Ameche,
Wisconsin Fullback

Over the seasons, there have been many marvelously descriptive nicknames attached to our gridiron heroes; Mr. Inside, Squirmin' Herman, The Iceman, Hopalong, Mr. Outside, The Golden Boy and The Magician to name but a few. The all-encompassing descriptor of the classic fullback belongs to but one man: Alan "The Horse" Ameche.

They hung the tag "The Horse" on Ameche the first afternoon he trotted onto the Wisconsin practice field, lined up and roared through the varsity '51 varsity line, knees pumping chin high and limbs knocking would-be tacklers akimbo. By the third game of his freshman season, young Alan showed more than enough to the Badger coaches. He replaced the Badger captain, Jim Hammond, at starting fullback.

Ameche, a former All Wisconsin high schooler from down-state Kenosha, not only started but started setting records immediately. He gained 824 yards in his first year for an average of 5.2 yards a carry. He led the Big Ten again in '52 and was third in '53, despite playing as a marked man in every game. His ability to play 55 minutes in the '53 season amplified his nickname: "The Iron Horse." An injury late in the '54

campaign cost him the iron part of his pseudonym and also prevented him from winning the rushing title again.

During Ameche's four seasons, Wisconsin was 26-8-3. In virtually every victory, his rushing was the top factor and he was seldom effectively stopped. After Wisconsin, Ameche went on to star for the Baltimore Colts. On his first NFL play, he ran 79 yards for a touchdown against the Chicago Bears. In the Colts' famous 23-17 overtime win over the New York Giants in the '58 title game, he scored the winning TD.

1954 Season Statistics:

Rush: 146   Yds: 641   TD: 9
Runners-Up: 2. Kurt Burris, Oklahoma
3. Howard Cassady, Ohio State
4. Ralph Guglielmi, Notre Dame
5. Paul Larson, California
6. Dick Moegel, Rice
7. Jack Elena, UCLA
8. George Shaw, Oregon
9. Pete Vann, Army
10. Bob McNamara, Minnesota

1955 Howard Cassady,
Ohio State Halfback

What a difference a year makes. When Howard Cassady was a senior at Columbus Central High School in Ohio, he would sneak into Ohio Stadium to watch the Buckeyes play. The following year, he earned a seat on the Buckeye bench for the season opener against Indiana. Then the 150-pound freshman was sent into the game. That afternoon he scored three touchdowns and led the Buckeyes to a 33-13 victory.

From then on, Howard "Hopalong" Cassady was a hometown hero in the OSU lineup, playing in 36 of a possible 37 games and leading the Buckeyes to a combined record of 29-8 over the next four years.

In '54, Cassady won unanimous All America honors, rushing for 701 yards and averaging 5.7 yards per carry. He also caught 13 passes for 148 yards in helping the Buckeyes to a perfect 10-0 record and the first of five national championships for Coach Woody Hayes. The '54 season concluded with a convincing 20-7 win over Southern California in the Rose Bowl.

Cassady again won All America acclaim in '55, when he rushed for 964 yards and 15 touchdowns.

At the end of the year, he not only won the Heisman but was also lauded by AP as the '55 Athlete of the Year. He also helped the Buckeyes earn another Top 10 national ranking. Their 7-2 record put them fifth.

Hopalong, who also was an outstanding defensive back, finished his collegiate career with 2,466 rushing yards. After graduation, he was a first round pick of the Detroit Lions. He played defensive back for Detroit, Cleveland and Philadelphia before retiring.

1955 Season Statistics:

Rush: 161   Yds: 958   TD: 15
Runners-Up: 2. Jim Swink, Texas Christian
3. George Welsh, Navy
4. Earl Morrall, Michigan State
5. Paul Hornung, Notre Dame
6. Bob Pellegrini, Maryland
7. Ron Beagle, Navy
8. Ron Kramer, Michigan
9. Bo Bolinger, Oklahoma
10. Jon Arnett, Southern California

1956 Paul Hornung,
Notre Dame Quarterback

There was only one quarterback in the history of the Heisman with enough personality, fame and talent to win the trophy after a losing season in which he passed for ... you ready for this? ... three touchdowns. And the people he beat that year? None less than such legends as John Majors of Tennessee, Jim Brown of Syracuse, Ron Kramer of Michigan, John Brodie of Stanford and Jim Parker of Ohio State.

Paul Hornung was known not just as Notre Dame's, but the nation's, Golden Boy. He did indeed play for a losing team; in '56, the Irish were pathetic. They were 2 and 8! To overcome those numbers and his Heisman competition, Hornung had to be an outstanding athlete.

He was. He played quarterback, fullback and safety. As a sophomore, he was a backup fullback and also averaged six points a game while earning a basketball monogram. As a junior, he finished fourth nationally in total offense with 1,215 yards and fifth in Heisman voting. In a '55 victory over then fourth-ranked Navy, he ran for one score, threw for another and intercepted two passes. Then he brought the Irish from behind against Iowa with a TD pass and game-

winning field goal in the final minutes. In a loss to USC, he threw and ran for 354 yards, an NCAA high that year.

Though he threw for only three TDs his senior year, Hornung did account for more than half the Irish scoring and ranked second nationally in total offense. A bonus pick of the Green Bay Packers, he starred at halfback and place kicker, leading the NFL in scoring in '59, '60 and '61. He entered the Pro Football Hall of Fame in '86.

1956 Season Statistics:

Att/Comp: 111/59   Yds: 917   TD: 3

Runners-Up:
2. Johnny Majors, Tennessee
3. Tommy McDonald, Oklahoma
4. Jerry Tubbs, Oklahoma
5. Jimmy Brown, Syracuse
6. Ron Kramer, Michigan
7. John Brodie, Stanford
8. Jim Parker, Ohio State
9. Kenny Ploen, Iowa
10. Joe Walton, Pittsburgh

1957 John David Crow,
Texas A&M Halfback

Every year a handful of young men emerge from high schools across the country as "can't miss" prospects coveted by scores of college coaches. They don't blossom and surprise. They're already there. They're expected to compete for the Heisman before they pull on a college jersey.

Such a stud back there in '53 was John David Crow of Springhill, Louisiana.

When the legendary coach, Paul "Bear" Bryant, left Kentucky to take on the Texas A&M job, his first mission was to recruit John David Crow. Bryant knew what he was doing. In his legendary career, John David — not Babe Parilli, Joe Namath, Ken Stabler, Steve Sloan, Johnny Musso nor John Hannah — was the only Heisman Trophy winner Bryant ever coached. He was both Consensus and Academic All America in '57.

From the beginning, Bryant expected Crow to win the Heisman. He was widely quoted in the newspapers as saying, "If John David doesn't win the Heisman, they ought to stop giving it." Years later, Crow admitted that he might not have won the trophy if it hadn't been for Bryant.

Bryant had unique respect for John David Crow. He

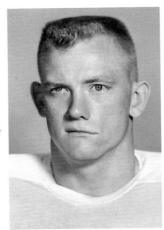

routinely called his players by their last name. But he made an exception for this pile-driving halfback. To Bryant, from high school on, Crow was always John David. Not John Crow or Johnny Crow or J.D. but John David.

At Bryant's funeral, Crow was describing what the trophy and Coach Bryant meant to him. "I cherish that Heisman Trophy," he said. "I'm proud that I'm the only one who ever played for Coach Bryant who won it. There will never be another one now, and I feel that's a great honor."

1957 Season Statistics:
Rush: 129   Yds: 562   TD: 10
Runners-Up: 2. Alex Karras, Iowa
3. Walt Kowalczyk, **Michigan State**
4. Lou Michaels, Kentucky
5. Tom Forrestal, Navy
6. Jim Phillips, Auburn
7. Bob Anderson, Army
8. Dan Currie, Michigan State
9. Clendon Thomas, Oklahoma
10. Lee Grosscup, Utah

1958 Pete Dawkins,
Army Halfback

They don't award the Heisman to coaches. If they did, a serious contender for it would have been Earl "Red" Blaik, the architect of a new era of football at West Point.

Blaik was coaching Dartmouth in the early '40s when he was offered the Army job. Before accepting, he proposed two conditions. One was that his Dartmouth staff be allowed to join him. The other was twofold: the liberalizing of height and weight restrictions that had been in place since the early '30s, and a change in limited football recruiting policies while still adhering to high scholastic and moral standards.

Under Blaik, Army compiled a 121-33-10 record. He remains the winningest coach in West Point history. Three of his teams were national champions, seven were crowned Lambert Trophy titlists, 28 Cadets were first team All Americans and three won the Heisman.

The last of Blaik's Heisman legends was Peter Dawkns, one of two first team All American halfbacks on the '58 Army team (Bob Anderson was the other and was also a '57 first team All American).

Dawkin's selection was far from a fluke. He had an

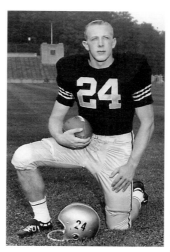

outstanding season and led Army to its last unbeaten season and Lambert Trophy. He also excelled in military and cadet training as well as in the classroom. He served as First Captain of the Corps of Cadets (the top cadet rank) during his senior year. He was also named to the Academic All America team. He became a Rhodes Scholar in '58 and while studying in England found time to not only master the game of Rugby but revolutionized it by teaching the old boys the intricacies of cutback rushing techniques.

1958 Season Statistics:

Rush: 78   Yds: 428   TD: 6

Runners-Up: 2. Randy Duncan, Iowa

3. Billy Cannon, Louisiana State

4. Bob White, Ohio State

5. Joe Kapp, California

6. Bill Austin, Rutgers

7. Bob Harrison, Oklahoma

8. Dick Bass, College of Pacific

9. Don Meredith,
Southern Methodist

10. Nick Pietrosante, Notre Dame

1959 Billy Cannon,
Louisiana State Halfback

College football programs don't tend to be cyclical. They get good and stay good for a period of years. Seldom does any school pop up out of nowhere and arrive in national prominence.

A major exception to this was the Louisiana State team of '59. After a No. 9 ranking in '49, LSU languished with also-rans for the next nine years, never making the Top 20, until the Tigers suddenly emerged as national champs in '58, the reward for a perfect 10-0 season.

A major reason for the Tigers' ascension to the top was halfback Billy Cannon. Even by today's – heck, tomorrow's – standards, this man was a rare athlete who combined sprinter speed with brute strength.

Cannon could consistently run a 9.5 in the 100-yard dash, which is outstanding for any human. At 6-1 and 210 pounds, it's nearly unheard of. Cannon had the size to overpower his opponents as well as the speed to outrun them. Big plays win Heismans and Cannon made them.

As a sophomore in '57, Cannon was an immediate

standout, both offensively and defensively. As a junior, he was the driving force behind the Fighting Tigers as they carved out a perfect season and captured the '58 national championship. To keep the season perfect, he passed for a touchdown and kicked the extra point in LSU's 7-0 win over Clemson in the Sugar Bowl, winning MVP honors in so doing.

LSU slumped to third in the country in '59 with a 9-1 record but Cannon repeated a remarkable year. Against third-ranked Ole Miss, LSU trailed 3-0. Early in the fourth quarter, Cannon took a punt and broke seven tackles on an 89-yard TD run, taking LSU to a 7-3 victory.

1959 Season Statistics:

Rush: 139   Yds: 598   TD: 6
Runners-Up: 2. Rich Lucas, Penn State
3. Don Meredith,
Southern Methodist
4. Bill Burrell, Illinois
5. Charles Flowers, Mississippi

1960

Joe Bellino,

Navy Halfback

He came from Winchester, Mass. and they called him the Winchester Rifle, the "player who was never caught from behind."

He was only 5-9 and 181 pounds, and he played when players went both ways. Lack of height didn't deter him a whit as he set 15 Naval Academy football records. He scored 31 touchdowns, rushed for 1,664 yards on 330 carries and returned 38 kicks for 833 more yards.

Bellino had the legs of a giant. His calves were as thick as some men's thighs. Once, after a 50-yard touchdown run against Boston College in the '59 season opener, he began to limp and fell to the ground. The trainer rushed out to the field to discover that the problem was the elastic rims on top of the high stockings the Midshipmen were wearing for the first time. Bellino's feet had turned blue from lack of circulation. The socks were cut and Bellino was good to go.

Bellino was a unanimous All America selection in '60 and also won the Maxwell Award. Again, a big play helped nail down the Heisman. Bellino's end zone interception preserved Navy's 17-12 over Army. Behind Bellino, the Midshipmen finished 4th in the polls with a 9-1 record and were invited to play in the Orange Bowl on Jan. I, '61.

Army fans can hardly forget the '59-'60 seasons for what Bellino did to the Cadets. He scored three touchdowns in the '59 Army-Navy football game and was equally sensational in their annual June baseball game in '60. The Cadets had just won the Eastern League when catcher Bellino went 4-4, threw out two runners and drove in three runs. Navy won, 9-1.

1960 Season Statistics:

Rush: 168   Yds: 834   TD: 18
Runners-Up: 2. Tom Brown, Minnesota
3. Jake Gibbs, Mississippi
4. Ed Dyas, Auburn
5. Bill Kilmer, UCLA

1961

Ernie Davis,
Syracuse Halfback

It took the voters of the Heisman 26 long seasons to recognize the prowess of the black athlete in college football. That's right. The first 26 winners were all white.

You'd think that among Jim Brown, Cookie Gilchrist and Ernie Davis the Heisman voters would find at least one black running back (and one Syracuse Orangeman) worthy of Heisman status. And though Jim Brown could only muster enough votes to finish fifth to Paul Hornung, John Majors and two Oklahoma Sooners in 1956, it was he who was responsible for Syracuse's and Africa-America's first Heisman winner. It was Brown who recruited Ernie Davis to Syracuse.

Davis did not disappoint Brown nor the Heisman selectors. He was so good in '62, they had to vote for him. At 6-1 and 212, he was the perfect halfback size. Plus he had outstanding speed. He was far and away the best back in the country, maybe even better than his predecessor, Jim Brown. He broke Brown's Syracuse records, setting new school career records for total rushing yards, rushing average (6.6) and

most TDs.

Davis led the Orangemen to an undefeated season, their first and only national championship plus a win over Texas in the Cotton Bowl. He then became the No. 1 pick in the '62 NFL draft. He was chosen by the Cleveland Browns who wanted to put him in the backfield with his friend from Syracuse, Jim Brown.

Most unfortunately, David did not make it to the Browns. At the '63 College All Star Game in Chicago, doctors discovered he had leukemia. He died the following May. The news of his death saddened all America.

1961 Season Statistics:
Rush: 150   Yds: 823   TD: 15
Runners-Up: 2. Bob Ferguson, Ohio State
3. Jimmy Saxton, Texas
4. Sandy Stephens, Minnesota
5. Pat Trammel, Alabama

1962 Terry Baker,
Oregon State Quarterback

While it took the voters of the Heisman 26 long seasons to honor black athletes, it took even longer to realize great football was played out west, even though 11 western teams had gone unbeaten since the Heisman's beginning and the Pac 10 was on the verge of taking 19 of the next 25 Rose Bowls from the midwest's mighty Big 10.

It was Terry Baker of previously unheralded Oregon State who paved the way for western Heismen, and he did it on sheer ability, not on trumped-up hype. He overcame regional favoritism by having such a spectacular season, Sports Illustrated twice put him on its cover in '62: once to proclaim him "The best athlete in college" and again to name him "Sportsman of the Year." He is the only Heisman winner to play in basketball's Final Four. In total, Baker collected 26 individual trophies to adorn his den in later years, including "Football Player of the Year" by both AP and UPI. And that's not counting the 12 different All America teams he was named to as their first string quarterback.

Baker accomplished all this on the second best team in the west. No. 1 was also the nation's No. 1 (that would be Southern California, who enjoyed a 11-0 season, including a 42-37 whipping of Wisconsin in the '63 Rose Bowl). Oregon State finished tied with Northwestern for 16th.

Baker was a left-handed QB and a right-handed pitcher and a guard on the OSU basketball team. He was a great runner; as a sophomore, he rushed 610 yards while throwing for 863. In his Heisman-winning season, he ran for 538 yards to complement a 1,738-yard passing year. Against ... he ran for 145 yards and passed for 107. ... ar college career, he ran for 1,503 yards ... d passed for another 3,476.

1962 Season Statistics:

Att/Comp: 203/112 Yds: 1,738 TD: 15
Runners-Up: 2. Jerry Stovall, Louisiana State
3. Bob Bell, Minnesota
4. Lee Roy Jordan, Alabama
5. George Mira, Miami

1963 Roger Staubach,
Navy Quarterback

Quick now. Unbeaten Texas was No. 1 in the country in '63 and Illinois was third. Who was second?

If you guessed Navy you're among a few who would have. Since World War II, Navy has not been noted for football powerhouses and has beaten Army only four times in the last 14 seasons.

However, '63 was Navy's year. Under Coach Wayne Hardin, Navy had but one loss in the regular season, to Southern Methodist, 32-28, and was gunning for the national championship as late as New Year's Day, '64. (Texas won that one, 28-6.)

There was another fellow who had something to do with Navy's outstanding '63 season: Roger "The Dodger" Staubach, a man who has scrambled his way to success as a college athlete, All-Pro NFL quarterback and respected businessman.

Like his Heisman predecessor Joe Bellino, Staubach was a complete athlete. He enjoyed a standout sophomore season and was only a junior when he won the Heisman. Among Navy's and Roger's victims

that year were West Virginia, Michigan, Notre Dame, Maryland and Army.

By the end of his college career, Staubach owned 28 Naval Academy records in football, despite being hampered by injuries his senior season. He also lettered in baseball three years as an outfielder and pitcher and won one letter in basketball.

A four-year hitch in Navy active duty did not diminish Staubach's abilities. In a brilliant pro football career, he directed the Dallas Cowboys to 23 fourth-quarter comeback wins.

1963 Season Statistics:
Att/Comp: 161/107   Yds: 1,474   TD: 7
Runners-Up: 2. Billy Lothridge, Georgia Tech
3. Sherman Lewis, Michigan State
4. Don Trull, Baylor
5. Scott Appleton, Texas

1964 John Huarte,
Notre Dame Quarterback

The year 1964 was a bumper crop in college football and a tough year for Heisman pickers. Dick Butkus was at Illinois, Jerry Rhome at Tulsa, Bob Timberlake at Michigan, Tucker Frederickson at Auburn, Craig Morton at Cal, Steve DeLong at Tennessee, Cosmo Iacavazzi at Princeton, Brian Piccolo at Wake Forest and John Huarte and Jack Snow at Notre Dame.

The vote was close, with Huarte edging Rhome by a scant 74 votes. Butkus finished a strong third, one of the highest placings ever by an interior lineman.

Californian Jack Snow to throw to and Snow nabbed 60 of his passes, a record nine for touchdowns. Huarte finished the year ranked third in the country in total offense with 2,069 yards, with more than half of those going to Snow (1,114 yards). Huarte set 12 Irish records and won player of the year honors from UPI. After college, he was a second draft choice of the Jets and played for six different teams in the pros for eight seasons.

Huarte's win ranks as one of the biggest upsets in the history of the award, considering he missed much of his sophomore season due to an injury and didn't play enough as a junior to win a monogram.

Huarte, who high schooled at renowned Mater Dei High in Santa Ana, California, owed his remarkable comeback to first-year Notre Dame Coach Ara Parseghian. The former Northwestern mentor turned Notre Dame from a 2-7 team in '63 into a 9-1 squad that came within minutes of a national title.

Huarte was but one of the Irish stars. He had fellow

1964 Season Statistics:

Att/Comp: 205/114   Yds: 2,062   TD: 16
Runners-Up: 2. Jerry Rhome, Tulsa
3. Dick Butkus, Illinois
4. Bob Timberlake, Michigan
5. Jack Snow, Notre Dame
6. Tucker Frederickson, Auburn
7. Craig Morton, California
8. Steve DeLong, Tennessee
9. Cosmo Iacavazzi, Princeton
10. Brian Piccolo, Wake Forest

1965

Mike Garrett,
Southern California Tailback

Three years after Ernie Davis became the first African-American to win the Heisman and two years after Terry Baker was the first west coaster to win it, a fellow showed up in the Southern California backfield to gloriously upgrade a USC tradition of change.

The USC Trojan legacy actually began way back in '25, a time when most U.S. colleges were segregated. Most football squads were all white and would be for decades to come. That year, USC produced its first All American, a black center named Brice Taylor. Several dozen All Americans later, Mike Garrett showed up and made All America at a new position: tailback.

That was '63. The next two years, Garrett again performed brilliantly and could not be denied by anybody who knew a football from a turnip. He made a couple of the All America teams in '64 and then in '65 the 185-pounder from Los Angeles led the nation with 1,440 yards.

Garrett was named first string on 11 All America

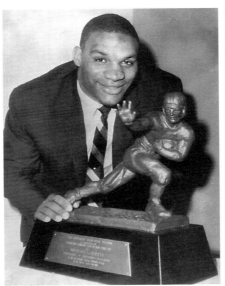

teams in '65, establishing a great legacy of USC I-formation tailbacks. USC had great All American backs before Garrett – Jon Arnett, Frank Gifford, Cotton Warburton and Erny Pinckert to name a few – but none of those were tailbacks and none won the Heisman.

Mike set 14 NCAA, conference and USC records in his three-year career, including an NCAA career rushing record of 3,221 yards in the days when 1,000-yards-a-season rushers were almost non-existent.

Mike later starred for the Kansas City Chiefs and San Diego Chargers. He was named USC's sixth-ever athletic director in '93.

1965 Season Statistics:

Rush: 267   Yds: 1,440   TD: 16
Runners-Up: 2. Howard Twilley, Tulsa
3. Jim Grabowski, Illinois
4. Don Anderson, Texas Tech
5. Floyd Little, Syracuse

1966 Steve Spurrier,
Florida Quarterback

This was the year that began a remarkable string of Heisman runners-up. In four consecutive years, three different Purdue backs would finish second in the Heisman.

In '66, it was quarterback Bob Griese's turn. Griese had a great career at Purdue, but at least there's consolation in knowing that he got beaten by the beginning of a Major College Football Dynasty, a rare and elite distinction officially classified by none less than the NCAA.

Before Steve Spurrier, Florida and Football Dynasty weren't synonymous. Starting with an end, Dale VanSickel, back in '28 (this guy went on to become one of Hollywood's leading stunt men), Florida had produced but five All Americans in its first 60 seasons. Spurrier changed that; first as a player, later as a coach. With Spurrier at the helm, the Gators are currently averaging nearly five All Americans a year!

Until Spurrier arrived, the Gators were seldom in the national rankings. With Spurrier as their quarterback, they popped up at No. 13 with a 7-3 record in '65 and moved up on an 8-2 season to

11th place in '66.

Spurrier was a two-time All American for the Gators and the SEC player of the year in '66. That year, he broke every school record for game, season and career in passing and total offense, and all league records for passing. He was the first losing player in the history of the Sugar Bowl to win MVP honors. That was in '66 when he set six game records in a 20-18 loss to Missouri. Spurrier had a great pro career, then signed on as Florida's coach on the last day of '89. His '90 team started the season 9-1 and the Gators have been winning ever since.

1966 Season Statistics:

Att/Comp: 291/179   Yds: 2,012   TD: 16
Runners-Up: 2. Bob Griese, Purdue
3. Nick Eddy, Notre Dame
4. Gary Beban, UCLA
5. Floyd Little, Syracuse

1967

Gary Beban,
UCLA Quarterback

Gary Beban's experience at beautiful UCLA in Westwood, California is exemplary of how a young American male should spend the final years of his teens. Everything about it is absolutely perfect.

Gary won the starting quarterback for the Bruins in his sophomore year in '65 and led the Bruins to a Rose Bowl victory in nearby Pasadena over the Big 10's mighty Michigan State and to wire service rankings of No. 4 and No. 5. The Bruins finished 8-2-1 on the year as Beban completed 78 of 152 passes for 1,483 yards and nine touchdowns. In the Rose Bowl clinching win over rival USC, Beban threw two touchdown passes in the final four minutes for a come-from-behind 20-16 victory. After that game, they nicknamed him "The Great One."

Just imagine strolling across the UCLA campus for two wonderful years and have one and all hail you: "Yo! Hello there, oh Great One."

As a junior, Beban led UCLA to a 9-1 record and another No. 5 ranking. That year, he completed 78 of 157 passes for 1,245 yards and six touchdowns. The next year, he led the Bruins to a

7-2-1 record and a No. 10 ranking. He completed 87 more passes and eight more touchdowns. This year he was not as successful against USC as the Bruins lost 21-20. But in passing for 301 yards in the game, the second-highest total in school history at the time, he did well enough to retain his nickname.

At season's end, The Great One won the Maxwell Award, the National Football Foundation and Hall of Fame Scholar-Athlete award, the Columbus Touchdown Award, consensus All American honors and the Heisman. And he still had half a year left to stroll across campus.

1967 Season Statistics:

Att/Comp: 156/87   Yds: 1,359   TD: 8
Runners-Up: 2. O.J. Simpson,
                    Southern California
            3. Leroy Keyes, Purdue
            4. Larry Csonka, Syracuse
            5. Kim Hammond, Florida State
            6. Bob Johnson, Tennessee
            7. Granville Liggins, Oklahoma

1968 O.J. Simpson,
Southern California Tailback

He's probably the most notorious of all the Heisman winners, due in some measure to running through airports for the rental-car company and playing the buffoon detective in several movies but mostly because of his role in the longest-running live daytime TV show in the history of American television. Until then, he was an admired human.

Oh, O.J. was well-known as a footballer, too — famous enough to be on the cover of Sports Illustrated eight times.

He started his college football career in junior college, a pattern not uncommon in California. When he arrived at USC, he was more than an adequate replacement for the great Mike Garrett.

He was a unanimous choice at one of the halfback spots on the '67 All America teams and led the Trojans, along with fellow All Americans Ron Yary, Adrian Young and Tim Rossovich, to a 9-1 record and the national championship. He was the Heisman runner-up in '67.

USC fell to fourth in the national polls in '68 with a 9-1-1 record behind Ohio State, Penn State and Texas. But O.J. again starred, making all the All America teams. That season, he rushed for 1,709 yards, a regular season NCAA record for yards rushing (it has since been bettered). He also equalled or bettered 18 other NCAA, conference and USC records. He's a starter on Sport Illustrated's All Century team.

In '68, O.J. captured the Heisman by the most one-sided margin in history. He then played pro football. He set an NFL single season rushing record of 2,003 yards in '73 and finished an 11-year pro career as the second leading NFL career rusher.

1968 Season Statistics:

Rush: 383   Yds: 1,709   TD: 23
Runners-Up: 2. Leroy Keyes, Purdue
3. Terry Hanratty, Notre Dame
4. Ted Kwalick, Penn State
5. Ted Hendricks, Miami

1969

Steve Owens,
Oklahoma Fullback

Though not as dominating as they'd been under Coach Bud Wilkinson in the '50s, the Oklahoma Sooners under Coach Chuck Fairbanks ('67-'72) played a powerful caliber of football. Fairbanks had 24 All Conference players and nine All Americans in his tenure and won three Big Eight titles.

Outstanding runners were what the Sooners were noted for back then. Anybody who followed college football from the '50s until now still gets chills recalling the exploits of Buck McPhail, Billy Vessels, Tommy McDonald, Clendon Thomas, Joe Don Looney, Jim Grisham, Steve Owens and Greg Pruitt.

Owens broke into the Sooner backfield as a sophomore in '67. He rushed 190 times for 808 yards and scored 12 touchdowns. His 4.2-yard average per carry was indicative of the kind of Sooner runner he was destined to be; he finished his Sooner career at an impressive 4.3.

Owens became the Sooner workhorse back the next two seasons and was rewarded by receiving back-to-back consensus All America honors. He scored more touchdowns (56) during his career than

any other Sooner. He also holds records for most points scored in a season (138), accomplishing that during the '69 season. He also broke several national records during his career, including most rushing yards (3,867).

After his incredible career, Owens was awarded the Walter Camp Trophy as well as the Heisman. After playing for the Detroit Lions, he came home to his roots. He served as OU's Athletic Director from '96 to '98. He was inducted into the National Football Hall of Fame in '91.

1969 Season Statistics:

Rush: 358   Yds: 1,523   TD: 23
Runners-Up: 2. Mike Phipps, Purdue
3. Rex Kern, Ohio State
4. Archie Manning, Mississippi
5. Mike Reed, Penn State
6. Mike McCoy, Notre Dame
7. Jim Otis, Ohio State
8. Jim Plunkett, Stanford
9. Steve Kiner, Tennessee
10. Jack Tatum, Ohio State

1970 Jim Plunkett,
Stanford Quarterback

After having no winners for the first 27 years of the Heisman, the west coast suddenly had five in the next nine. Go figure.

Talent must have had something to do with it. And talent, especially quarterback talent, was something Stanford had long been famous for. Frankie Albert and John Brodie quickly come to mind. On September 21, '68, San Jose's Jim Plunkett was added to the list.

Plunkett's parents were of Mexican descent. His mother was blind. His father, a news vendor, had progressive blindness. The significance of all this is that Plunkett grew up poor but quite protective of his parents. The reason he chose to attend Stanford was so he could be near them.

Plunkett's first Stanford start in '68 set the pattern for three years of great offensive football. The young Mexican led the Indians to a 68-20 rout of the San Jose State Spartans and by the end of the season he threw for more yards than any player in the history of the Pac 8 (it didn't become the Pac 10 until the two Arizona teams joined).

By the time his junior season was in the record books, Plunkett was famous. He broke his own records, throwing 2,673 yards and 20 touchdowns. He had little left to prove and when the pros beckoned many reckoned he would make himself eligible for the draft. His response was the stuff that guarantees some payback: "We are always telling kids today not to drop out ... what would they think if I were to drop out for professional football?" Plunkett stayed in school, led the Indians to the '70 Pac 8 championship and a 27-17 upset over Ohio State in the '71 Rose Bowl. Of course he won the Heisman. This is what it's all about.

1970 Season Statistics:

Att/Comp: 358/191   Yds: 2,715   TD: 18
Runners-Up: 2. Joe Theismann, Notre Dame
3. Archie Manning, Mississippi
4. Steve Worster, Texas
5. Rex Kern, Ohio State

1971

Pat Sullivan,
Auburn Quarterback

It's often been said. Big plays in big games win Heismans. That's exactly what it took in '71, year of the closest Heisman vote in history.

Auburn had begun the year by beating Mississippi in the Gator Bowl, 35-28. Now here they were in Athens, Georgia, ten and a half months later on Nov. 13. The game was Auburn vs. Georgia. Never before had two undefeated Southeastern Conference teams met this late in the season. To the winner went the SEC championship, a trip to the Sugar Bowl, the Heisman for the Auburn quarterback if Auburn should win.

Georgia had given up only 20 points to five SEC foes going into the Auburn game. A week before, the Bulldogs beat Florida, 49-7. The Auburn Tigers had the Pat Sullivan-led offense. Only once had they come close to defeat, against Tennessee in Knoxville, when Sullivan had to lead the Tigers 86 yards to score a come-from-behind 10-9 victory in the last minutes of the game.

As Georgia was challenging Auburn, someone was challenging Sullivan for the Heisman: Ed Marinaro, a fullback from Cornell. Back east, writers were lining up to support both him and Ivy League football.

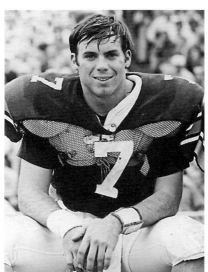

On that day, Sullivan rose to the occasion. He accounted for 57 yards in Auburn's first possession, a 62-yard drive for a TD. Next possession, he got 62 of a 63-yard drive for another TD. Just before the half, he was parallel to the ground when he threw a 15-yard TD pass to Dick Schmalz. Sullivan threw for two more TDs in the second half, one a 70-yarder to favorite receiver Terry Beasley. Auburn won 35-20. Twelve days later, the announcement was made. Sullivan won the Heisman.

1971 Season Statistics:

Att/Comp: 281/162   Yds: 2,012   TD: 20
Runners-Up: 2. Ed Marinaro, Cornell
3. Greg Pruitt, Oklahoma
4. John Musso, Alabama
5. Lydell Mitchell, Penn State
6. Jack Mildren, Oklahoma
7. Jerry Tagge, Nebraska
8. Chuck Ealey, Toledo
9. Walt Patulski, Notre Dame
10. Eric Allen, Michigan State

1972 Johnny Rodgers,
Nebraska Flanker

He was the Peter Warrick of his era. The difference between the two was that Johnny Rodgers confined his notoriety to the football field.

At the end of the twentieth century, Sports Illustrated ranked him the fifth best Nebraska athlete of the century, behind Bob Gibson, Gale Sayers, Grover Cleveland Alexander and Tom Osborne. The magazine also placed him on its All Century team.

Rodgers was every bit as electrifying as Warrick or anybody else who ever played the game. He delayed several Thanksgiving dinners; his nationally televised feats in Turkey Day Nebraska-Oklahoma games were classics.

Rodgers starred for three years for Nebraska and had much to do with Nebraska's lofty ranking those three years. The Cornhuskers won the national championship in '70 and '71 with unbeaten seasons and ranked fourth in '72 at 9-2-1. They were 33-2-2 with Rodgers at the wingback slot.

Rodgers was most dangerous as a punt and kickoff returner. He is also Nebraska's all-time leading receiver with 143 catches for 2,479 yards and is in the Top 5 in

career points with 270 on 45 touchdowns in his career.

At Nebraska, he returned seven punts and one kickoff for touchdowns, averaging 15.5 yards on punt returns and 24.2 yards on kickoff returns. He also rushed for 786 yards, averaging six yards a carry.

After winning the Heisman, Rodgers capped his brilliant career with an unbelievable Orange Bowl performance against Notre Dame. In the 40-6 NU victory, Rodgers scored four touchdowns and passed for a fifth.

1972 Season Statistics:

Att/Comp: Rec: 55   Yds: 942   TD: 17
Runners-Up: 2. *Greg Pruitt, Oklahoma*
3. *Rich Glover, Nebraska*
4. *Bert Jones, Louisiana State*
5. *Terry Davis, Alabama*
6. *John Hufnagel, Penn State*
7. *George Amundsen, Iowa State*
8. *Otis Armstrong, Purdue*
9. *Don Strock, Virginia Tech*
10. *Gary Huff, Florida State*

1973 John Cappelletti,
Penn State Halfback

One of the things that's hardest to believe about John Cappelletti, a man who is approaching his 50th birthday, is that his college football coach was Joe Paterno, the same Joe Paterno who is currently coaching Penn State.

Paterno owes his longevity at Penn State to one thing: success. His teams finished second in the nation in '68 and '69, 18th in '70, fifth in '71, 10th in '72, and fifth again in '73. By then, with that kind of success behind him, it was high time one of his players won the Heisman.

John Cappelletti was the man chosen for that honor. He set up his Heisman year by playing defensive back as a sophomore, then switched to offense his junior year and produced the third best year in Penn State history by gaining 1,117 yards rushing. In his senior year, he had the second best year in Penn State history. He rushed for 1,522 yards. In his two-year career as a ball carrier, he averaged 120 yards a game, 5.1 yards a carry and scored 29 touchdowns.

Cappelletti was named to virtually every All America team in '73. His acceptance speech at the Heisman Dinner (with Vice President Gerald Ford

seated next to him on the dais) was considered by Downtown Athletic Club hosts to be the most moving ever given at these ceremonies, as he honored his brother Joey, a victim of leukemia.

John was signed by the Rams (first round draft choice) and spent two years grinding out short yardage for them. He started for the Rams in '76 and rushed for 688 yards. He was then traded to the San Diego Chargers and retired from pro ball after the '83 season.

1973 Season Statistics:

Rush: 286   Yds: 1,522   TD: 17
Runners-Up: 2. John Hicks, Ohio State
3. Roosevelt Leaks, Texas
4. David Jaynes, Kansas
5. Archie Griffin, Ohio State
6. Randy Gradishar, Ohio State
7. Lucious Selmon, Oklahoma
8. Woody Green, Arizona State
9. Danny White, Arizona State
10. Kermit Johnson, UCLA

1974 Archie Griffin,
Ohio State Halfback

Ohio State has always had one of the best college football programs in the country. At the beginning of the '74 season, it was considered one of the best in history.

The Buckeyes had just gone 10-0-1 in '73. This included a 42-21 trouncing of USC in the Rose Bowl. OSU became the first school to own three of the top six vote-getters in the Heisman balloting. There were four Buckeye All Americans in '73: Van Ness DeCree at defensive end, John Hicks at offensive tackle, Randy Gradishar at linebacker and sophomore Archie Griffin at tailback. With five Big Ten titles, two national championships and four Rose Bowl trips all in a six-year span, Ohio State football popularity was at an all-time high. Columbus became known as the "Capital of College Football."

Griffin was the Buckeyes' starting tailback for four years, leading Ohio State to a 40-5-1 record and four Big Ten titles. He started in four consecutive Rose Bowls, the only player ever to do so, and was a three-time first-team All American.

At 5-9 and 180 pounds, Griffin was small by college football standards even then, but no football

accomplishment was beyond his reach.

In just the second game of his freshman year, Griffin ran for a school record 239 yards. It was the start of a brilliant career that would see him amass an OSU record of 5,589 yards and 26 touchdowns. Griffin's stats put him in very select company among NCAA ball carriers of all time. Over his four great seasons, he averaged 6.13 yards per carry.

1974 Season Statistics:

Rush: 256   Yds: 1,695   TD: 12
Runners-Up: 2. Anthony Davis,
Southern California
3. Joe Washington, Oklahoma
4. Tom Clements, Notre Dame
5. Dave Humm, Nebraska
6. Dennis Franklin, Michigan State
7. Rod Shoate, Oklahoma
8. Gary Scheide, Brigham Young
9. Randy White, Maryland
10. Steve Bartkowski, California

1975

Archie Griffin,
Ohio State Halfback

As the '75 college football season got under way, it appeared that only a major injury could prevent Archie Griffin from becoming the first player ever to win a second Heisman.

In '75 Griffin stayed healthy and both Griffin and the Buckeyes continued to roll. The Buckeyes even improved on their 10-2 record for '74, cruising through the '75 season at 11-1. The Buckeyes won their seventh Big Ten Championship in eight years and went to their fourth Rose Bowl in a row. This is where they got the loss; UCLA beat them 23-10.

It was to west coast reporters that Coach Woody Hayes gave a now famous quote about Griffin: "He's a better young man than he is a football player, and he's the best football player I've ever seen."

Many of the games Griffin played in were routs, yet he racked up awesome stats by rarely playing more than half a game. Coach Hayes always opted to take his star out as soon as the Buckeyes were in control. Despite limited playing time, Griffin became Ohio State's career rushing leader with total yardage of 5,589.

Between his sophomore and senior seasons, Griffin

ran for 100 or more yards in 31 consecutive regular-season games. That became an NCAA record. Following his senior year, Griffin received the NCAA's prestigious Top Five Award for combined excellence in athletics, academics and leadership. It is the highest award the NCAA can bestow.

After graduation, Griffin was a first-round draft choice of the Cincinnati Bengals. He played eight years of professional football before returning to Columbus and joining the staff at Ohio State.

1975 Season Statistics:

Rush: 262   Yds: 1,450   TD: 4
Runners-Up: 2. Chuck Muncie, California
3. Ricky Bell, Southern California
4. Tony Dorsett, Pittsburgh
5. Joe Washington, Oklahoma
6. Jimmy Dubose, Florida
7. John Sciarra, UCLA
8. Gordon Bell, Michigan
9. Lee Roy Selmon, Oklahoma
10. Gene Swick, Toledo

1976 Tony Dorsett,
Pittsburgh Halfback

The season before Tony Dorsett came to Pittsburgh the Panthers won one game. It was a very embarrassing time for Pitt graduates Joe Schmidt, Hugh Green, Marshall Goldberg, Johnny Majors and Mike Ditka. It is doubtful that any of them called sportswriters before the '73 season to reassure them that a skinny freshman tailback out of Hopewell High School in Aliquippa, Pennsylvania, would come lead the Panthers to a national championship, win the Heisman trophy and leave Pitt acclaimed as the greatest running back in the history of college football.

Tony Dorsett may have come out of nowhere, but he came out running hard. In Pitt's opening game in '73, he gained 100 yards against Georgia. For the season, he gained 1,586 yards, the most ever by a college freshman. He led Pitt to a 6-5-1 record and a trip to the Fiesta Bowl.

By the time he was a junior, he was really rolling. He rushed for 1,544 yards in the regular season, including a memorable 303-yard performance against Notre Dame.

In the final seven games of his senior season, as Pitt was charging toward the national championship, he averaged 215 yards rushing per game en route to leading the nation in rushing with 1,948 yards. Having finished fourth in the Heisman voting as a junior, Dorsett upped his chances his senior year by setting the NCAA career rushing record with 6,082 yards. Counting bowl games, the number is 6,526 yards.

Dorsett has the distinction of being the only football player to win the Heisman, a collegiate national football championship, a Super Bowl championship and to be elected into both the college and pro halls of fame.

1976 Season Statistics:

Rush: 370   Yards: 2,150   TD: 23
Runners-Up: 2. Ricky Bell, Southern California
3. Rob Lytle, Michigan
4. Terry Miller, Oklahoma State
5. Tom Kramer, Rice

1977 Earl Campbell,
Texas Fullback

He was born in Tyler, Texas in '55, one of the middle children (fifth) of the eleven raised by Ann Campbell. Eighteen years later, he and two of his six brothers, Tim and Steve, took off for Austin to claim a special place in the University of Texas football history.

The three brothers did make Mama Ann proud. Tim and Steve both won their letters and Earl made the history books instantly, starting at fullback in the Longhorn wishbone attack. He rushed for 928 yards and six touchdowns his freshman year and made the All-SWC team.

He did even better as a sophomore. He ran for 1,118 yards and 13 touchdowns, earning his first of two consensus All America awards. He led Texas to a 10-2 record that year and a No. 6 ranking in the AP poll.

Injuries dampened the glitter of the Campbell career in '76, as he missed four games with a pulled hamstring and the Longhorns struggled to a 5-5-1 mark.

By his senior season, Campbell was at full strength and again was a consensus All American. He finished

his brilliant career with a Longhorn record 4,443 yards and 41 touchdowns. That season, he was the NCAA rushing, scoring and all-purpose yardage champion. And the Longhorns were national champs.

After winning the Heisman, Campbell was drafted No. 1 by the Houston Oilers and made a name for himself in the pros in a hurry. As a rookie, he claimed virtually every award possible including rookie of the year, most valuable offensive player and league MVP. He was voted into the NFL's Hall of Fame in '91.

1977 Season Statistics:

Rush: 267 Yards: 1,744 TD: 19
Runners-Up: 2. Terry Miller, Oklahoma State
3. Ken MacAfee, Notre Dame
4. Doug Williams,
Grambling College
5. Ross Browner, Notre Dame

1978 Billy Sims,
Oklahoma Halfback

In the seventies, nobody played better football than Oklahoma. Between '70 and '80 the Sooners were out of the Top 10 only once (20th in '70) and chalked up a seventh, a fifth, four thirds, two seconds and two national championships. In that era, dozens of Sooners made All Big Eight and no less than 31 made All America.

The Sooners were so good and so deep back then, a Sooner's best competition was from his own teammates. It was often said that Oklahoma's second string was good enough to be in the Top 10. In '75, the year Billy Sims joined the Sooners, eight Sooners made All America.

Sims was good enough to get into a few games in his freshman season, then had a sensational sophomore start, averaging 14.6 yards a carry. Unfortunately, he got hurt and only carried three times that year. He was given hardship ruling and had three years of eligibility left. He got only only 65 carries in '77 but averaged 6.2 yards a carry and was destined for greatness in '78 and '79.

The fourth-year junior from Hooks, Texas, thundered through 12 big-time defenses in '78. He set a Big Eight single season rushing record with 1,762 yards on only 231 carries. He averaged an

astounding 7.6 yards a carry and led the nation in rushing. He was the only back among the top 50 to average over 7.0. He also topped the 200-yard mark in four different games (a school best) during the '78 season.

OU's only loss in '78 was in the regular-season rivalry with Nebraska, 17-14. Sims led the Sooners to an 11-1 record, a national ranking of third and a rematch win over Nebraska in the Orange Bowl, 31-24.

1978 Season Statistics:

Rush: 231   Yards: 1,762   TD: 20
Runners-Up: 2. Chuck Fusina, Penn State
3. Rick Leach, Michigan
4. Charles White, Southern California
5. Charles Alexander, Louisiana State
6. Ted Brown, North Carolina State
7. Steve Fuller, Clemson
8. Eddie Lee Ivery, Georgia Tech
9. Jack Thompson, Washington State
10. Jerry Robinson, UCLA

1979 Charles White,
Southern California Tailback

Billy Sims had another great year in '79, but Charles White's season was even more awesome. After leading the Trojans to the national championship (UPI poll) in '78, White really went to work in '79. He rushed 108 times more than Sims and outgained the '78 Heisman winner by 297 yards in leading the Trojans to an 11-0-1 season. USC finished second in the nation in '79 with Oklahoma at third with an 11-1 record.

White was the fifth USC tailback in 15 years to finish first or second in Heisman voting. He was extremely durable and versatile. Coach John Robinson separated him from his other great tailbacks by claiming, "He's the most competitive athlete I've ever seen." As USC's all-purpose back, he averaged 30 to 40 carries a game. In the nationally televised 42-23 win over Notre Dame, he carried 44 times for 261 yards and four touchdowns.

White finished his four-year career as the NCAA's second leading rusher ever with 5,598 regular season yards. Including bowl games, he finished with a Pac-10 record 6,245.

A two-time unanimous All American, White set or equaled 22 NCAA, Pac-10, USC and Rose Bowl records. He gained over 100 yards 31 times in his career, including 10 times out of 12 games in '79. In his Heisman-winning season, White averaged 186.4 yards a game, 6.2 yards a carry, led the nation in rushing, and, for the second straight season, led it in all-purpose running.

In his final college game, the '80 Rose Bowl, White stole the show, gaining 247 yards in a come-from-behind 17-16 win over Ohio State.

1979 Season Statistics:

Rush: 332   Yards: 1,803   TD: 19
Runners-Up: *2. Billy Sims, Oklahoma*
         3. Marc Wilson, Brigham Young
         4. Art Schlichter, Ohio State
         5. Vagas Ferguson, Notre Dame
         6. Paul McDonald,
           Southern California
         7. George Rogers, South Carolina
         8. Mark Herrmann, Purdue
         9. Ron Simmons, Florida State
         10. Steadman Shealy, Alabama

1980

George Rogers,
South Carolina Tailback

In '80, another USC tailback joined the most illustrious list of runners in college football history. The difference was, this one was not from the University of Southern California but from South Carolina.

Until George Rogers came along, this USC was known for perennial mediocrity. Before Rogers, USC's only other eight-plus-win season was back in '03, when the schedule included two YMCAs and a high school team. And Rogers led his USC mates to two eight-plus-win seasons.

As sad as the past was for South Carolina, it was even more grim for young Mr. Rogers. He was born into a poor black family in Atlanta and his parents were separated when he was five. His father later went to prison on a murder charge. When Rogers was 13, he skipped classes to stack sacks of cement for $1.80 an hour to help support his family.

Never in the history of the Heisman has there been a more dramatic poverty-to-riches transition. In four years at USC, Rogers not only changed South Carolina football but also put his name in the NCAA

record books. His career rushing total of 4,498 yards put the 6-2, 224-pounder at No. 4 on the all-time NCAA rushing list, behind former Heisman winners Tony Dorsett, Charles White and Archie Griffin.

As Rogers racked up the yards, he also put more than a few bruises on USC opponents. He was bigger than any of the abovementioned Heisman winners, but this USC runner – "rolling thunder," one local writer called him – was just as fast, timed at 4.47 in the 40-yard dash. That combination of speed and size made him hard to catch, harder still to bring down. When he graduated, more than a few tears were shed. And wouldn't USC and Lou Holtz love to have the likes of him today?

1980 Season Statistics:

Rush: 324   Yds: 1,894   TD: 14
Runners-Up: 2. *Hugh Green, Pittsburgh*
              3. *Herschel Walker, Georgia*
              4. *Mark Herrmann, Purdue*
              5. *Jim McMahon, Brigham Young*

1981

Marcus Allen,
Southern California Tailback

They called '78 Heisman winner Billy Sims a workhorse back and that he was. But three years later, Marcus Allen nearly doubled Billy's carries in a season, 433 to 231. And Allen carried 101 times more than another great USC record setter, Charles White.

Allen was a sophomore when White did nearly all the rushing for the Trojans in '79. He learned well, piling up 624 more yards in '81 than White did when he won the Heisman in '79.

From '62 to '90, USC had at least one first team All American every year. Between Allen and Frank Gifford in '51, no less than 14 Trojans backs made All America. They were all great backs, but they also had some help. From '64 until now, there have been an amazing 26 first team All American Trojan offensive linemen.

Notwithstanding the benefits of another great Trojan line and an apprenticeship under Heisman winner Charles White, Allen had an incredible '81 season. He was college football's first 2,000-yard rusher, beating that mark by 427 yards.

Allen set 14 new NCAA records in '81 and tied two others, including the season rushing mark (bowl included) of 2,427, highest per-game average (212.9), most 200-yard games in a career (11), most 200-yard games in a season (8) and most most 200-yard games in a row (5).

Allen was drafted in the first round by the Oakland Raiders in '82 and retired from the Kansas City Chiefs after the '97 season. His pro honors include MVP of the Super Bowl and the NFL. He is the leading rusher in Raider history.

1981 Season Statistics:

Rush: 433   Yards: 2,427   TD: 23
Runners-Up: 2. Herschel Walker, Georgia
3. Jim McMahon, Brigham Young
4. Dan Marino, Pittsburgh
5. Art Schlichter, Ohio State

1982 Herschel Walker,
Georgia Tailback

Herschel Walker was a hypester's dream. They cranked out superlatives on him that would go beyond hyperbole on other mortal beings.

Herschel had the stats. A 6-1, 222-pound tailback from Wrightsville, he rushed for 3,167 yards and 45 TDs in his senior year at Georgia's Johnson County High, adding to the 41 TDs he had previously scored. A consensus high school All American, PARADE Magazine named him "National High School Back of the Year."

He also excelled in track. He ran the hundred in 9.5 and the 220 in 21.5. You think he wasn't recruited by more than a few colleges? When he decided on Georgia, the governor considered declaring a state holiday to mark the miracle.

The new Bulldog did not disappoint. He had the best freshman season a college back ever had. The Bulldogs were national champs. He set a new NCAA freshman rushing record (1,616 yards) and was the first freshman to be named All America by the Football Writers Association of America. He also

starred in NCAA indoor and outdoor track.

It was same-old, same-old his sophomore and junior years. He was the consensus All America tailback and finished second and then beat out Stanford's John Elway for the '82 Heisman, racking up the third most rushing yards in NCAA history, 5,259. After 32 games, he had 50 TDs.

With little left to prove, Herschel left Georgia and signed with the New Jersey Generals of the United States Football League. He joined the NFL in '86 and in '89 the Dallas Cowboys geared up for future Super Bowls by trading him to the Minnesota Vikings for five players and eight high draft choices.

1935 Season Statistics:

Rush: 335   Yards: 1,752   TD: 17
Runners-Up: 2. John Elway, Stanford
3. Eric Dickerson,
Southern Methodist
4. Anthony Carter, Michigan
5. Dave Rimington, Nebraska

1983 Mike Rozier,
Nebraska Halfback

When Herschel Walker opted to turn pro after his junior year at Georgia, the Heisman voters scoured the country for other candidates for the '83 award.

Not surprisingly, much of their focus was on what was happening at the University of Nebraska's Memorial Stadium. This hallowed arena had long been a hotbed for Heisman hopefuls. No less than 14 Heisman winners have played there during their collegiate careers, including the first Heisman winner, Chicago's Jay Berwanger and the first Nebraska winner, Johnny Rodgers.

A player named Mike Rozier first showed indications that he was in the running in his sophomore year. Rozier averaged 6.2 yards a carry in '81, racking up 943 yards and scoring five touchdowns.

As a junior, he started an assault on Nebraska and Big Eight records. That year, he averaged seven yards a carry and upped his rushing total to 1,689 yards. He also helped Nebraska move up in the polls, all the way to third with a record of 12-1 (in '83, the 12-1 Cornhuskers made it to No. 2).

In his senior season, Rozier was awesome. He came close to averaging a first down per carry (7.8 yards) on the way to piling up 2,148 yards. For his Cornhusker career, he scored 52 touchdowns. His gaudy rushing stats were enhanced by 216 receiving yards (10.8 average) and 449 yards on kick returns (22.5 average).

Of all the Heisman legends who've trod Memorial Stadium turf, Mike's traveled the farthest. He set the all-time Nebraska scoring and rushing scoring records before joining the Houston Oilers in '84.

1983 Season Statistics:

Rush: 275   Yards: 2,148   TD: 29
Runners-Up: 2. Steve Young, Brigham Young
3. Doug Flutie, Boston College
4. Turner Gill, Nebraska
5. Terry Hoage, Georgia

1984 Doug Flutie,
Boston College Quarterback

There was one big reason why Boston College won 10 games in '84 and finished fifth in the nation, the highest ranking ever for them. That was the little fellow at quarterback, the indomitable Doug Flutie.

There are thousands of football fans (the author included) who remember exactly where they were watching television the moment Flutie threw THE 48-yard touchdown pass with no time left on the clock that gave Boston College a 47-45 victory over the '83 national champions, the Miami Hurricanes. That play ranks as one of the most thrilling in college football history. Other highlights of Flutie's senior season include two touchdown passes on fourth-down plays to lead the Eagles to a 38-31 comeback win over the Alabama Crimson Tide at Birmingham ... six touchdown passes in a 52-20 romp over North Carolina ... 472 yards against Miami on 34 out of 46 with no interceptions ... and a career total of 1,420 yards against Joe Paterno's Penn State Nittany Lions.

It was nearly impossible to deny Flutie the Heisman in '84. En route to the winning trophy, he set the all-

time major college career passing record (10,579 yards) and the all-time major college career total offense record (11,054 yards). He not only made the Kodak All America team, they made him the captain.

Flutie's scholastic achievement was also recognized. He received a National Football Foundation post-graduate scholarship and was nominated as a candidate for the Rhodes Scholarship by Boston College.

At age 38, the little man with the big arm was still slinging footballs — for the Buffalo Bills of the National Football League.

1984 Season Statistics:

Att/Comp: 396/233   Yds: 3,454   TD: 27
Runners-Up: 2. Keith Byars, Ohio State
3. Robbie Bosco, Brigham Young
4. Bernie Kosar, Miami
5. Ken Davis, Texas Christian

1985 Bo Jackson,
Auburn Halfback

Bo Jackson was another mortal blessed with unbelievably superior talent. Bo was discovered by Auburn assistant Bobby Wallace when he was a high school junior in Bessemer, Alabama. According to Wallace, "I quickly realized he was a tremendous athlete. I told Coach Pat Dye I thought Bo was another Herschel Walker."

Wallace was right. Jackson made an immediate impact at Auburn. During initial fall practices in '82, he averaged 12 yards a carry.

As a freshman in the Southeastern Conference, Jackson was Auburn's leading rusher with 829 yards on 127 carries (6.5 yards per carry). His biggest contribution that first year came against rival Alabama. He scored the winning touchdown in a 23-22 victory, a run that ended a nine-game winning streak by Alabama. Coach Dye credits that run for "making Auburn people believe they could be good." By the end of his Auburn career, Jackson owned virtually every Auburn rushing record. He made the All America teams in '83 and '85 and beat out Iowa quarterback Chuck Long by 46 votes to win the '85

Heisman in the closest vote in the history of the award.

Jackson also made an impact in Tiger baseball and track and became the first three-sport letterman in the SEC in 20 years. He surprised a lot of people when he signed a professional baseball contract upon leaving Auburn. He made it to the big leagues in only one year and became a feared hitter with Kansas City. He was MVP of the '89 baseball All Star game. He also played pro football "as a hobby." But he played it well enough to lead the Oakland Raiders in rushing and make All Pro.

1985 Season Statistics:

Rush: 278   Yards: 1,786   TD: 17
Runners-Up: 2. Chuck Long, Iowa
3. Robbie Bosco, Brigham Young
4. Lorenzo White, Michigan State
5. Vinny Testaverde, Miami

1986 Vinny Testaverde,
Miami (FL) Quarterback

In the decade of the 80's, a new power emerged in college football. In a 10-year run, from '83 to '92, the University of Miami Hurricanes won four national championships, finished second twice and third twice. It was definitely one of the greatest decades for a team in college football history.

Obviously, the Hurricanes featured some outstanding football players during that streak. They were especially strong at quarterback. In addition to Heisman candidates Bernie Kosar and Steve Walsh, the Hurricanes also produced a couple of Heisman winners: Vinny Testaverde in '86 and Gino Torretta in '92.

Testaverde was a Kosar understudy. The 6-5, 218 pounder from Elmont, New York was rated as one of the finest ever to play at his position in the college game. When Kosar graduated and Testaverde got his chance, he made the most of it. He finished fifth in '85 Heisman voting before winning it the following year. The fifth-year senior won everything else that year, including the Maxwell Award, the Davey O'Brien Award, Walter Camp Player of the Year, Washington D.C. Touchdown Club Athlete of the

Year and consensus All American. He showed enough to get his jersey number retired.

Besides having phenomenal size and talent, Testaverde also used a tremendous work ethic in the strength and conditioning room to achieve success. He was also a superior student of the game. His ability to master the complex UM offensive scheme was a major factor in Miami's gaudy record of 21-2 in the two seasons he was at the helm.

1986 Season Statistics:

Att/Comp: 276/175   Yds: 2,557   TD: 26
Runners-Up: 2. Paul Palmer, Temple
           3. Jim Harbaugh, Michigan
           4. Brian Bosworth, Oklahoma
           5. Gordon Lockbaum, Holy Cross
           6. Brent Fullwood, Auburn
           7. Cornelius Bennett, Alabama
           8. D.J. Dozier, Penn State
           9. Kevin Sweeney, Fresno State
          10. Chris Spielman, Ohio State

1987

Tim Brown,
Notre Dame Wide Receiver

The year 1987 was a banner year for NFL recruiters. The 10 finalists in Heisman voting that year read like a Who's Who in pro football for the next decade. The list included Florida's Emmitt Smith, Oklahoma State's Thurman Thomas, Ohio State's Chris Spielman, Pittsburgh's Craig Heyward, Don McPherson of Syracuse and the All American soon to be All Pro, Tim Brown of Notre Dame.

Brown burst onto the national scene in his junior with a scintillating season-ending performance in a come-from-behind upset of USC, then used back-to-back punt returns for touchdowns in an early-season '87 game against Michigan State to cement his Heisman bid. Listed as a flanker, Brown utilized his ability as a pass receiver, rusher out of a full-house backfield and punt and kickoff returner to rank third nationally in all-purpose yardage as a junior (176.5 per game) and sixth as a senior (167.9).

In that memorable USC game in his junior year, he gained 254 all-purpose yards in Notre Dame's 38-37 win. The game was nationally televised and by the time it was over Brown was a Heisman candidate. His heroics

included a last-minute 56-yard punt return that set up the winning field goal.

Against Michigan State, he returned punts for TDs on runs of 66 and 71 yards to lead the Irish to a romp over the team that went on to be the Big 10 and Rose Bowl champs. Despite double and triple coverage, he was the most dangerous player in college football. He then became a perennial All Pro with the Raiders of Los Angeles and Oakland.

1987 Season Statistics:

Rec: 39   Yds: 846   TD: 7
Runners-Up: 2. *Don McPherson, Syracuse*
3. *Gordie Lockbaum, Holy Cross*
4. *Lorenzo White, Michigan State*
5. *Craig Heyward, Pittsburgh*
6. *Chris Spielman, Ohio State*
7. *Thurman Thomas,*
Oklahoma State
8. *Gaston Green, UCLA*
9. *Emmitt Smith, Florida*
10. *Bobby Humphrey, Alabama*

1988 Barry Sanders,
Oklahoma State Running Back

As great as Barry Sanders was, he could have owned nearly every record in the books for both college and pro running backs. Just before establishing all-time records, he walked away from both his college and pro careers.

By the end of his junior year at Oklahoma State, Sanders had set or tied 24 NCAA records. He was one TD short of the most TDs and points in a career, with a full season to go. He forfeited that season and turned pro. Then, needing one good season to break Walter Payton's all-time NFL career rushing record, he up and retired from the game.

He still made history, season after season. And there aren't enough superlatives to describe his '88 Oklahoma State season. He started it as Thurman Thomas' replacement at tailback and an All American kick returner. He ended it as a runaway Heisman winner and the most exciting football player in America.

He established a new standard for college runners. He gained 157 yards against Texas A&M, and that was his low for the season. In setting a new single-

season rushing mark previously held by USC's Marcus Allen, he was so consistently awesome he was named Big Eight Conference Player of the Week an unprecedented seven times. He rushed for more than 300 yards four times and eclipsed the 200-yard mark two additional times.

These are stats that attracted him to the pros: In the '88 season, he averaged 7.6 yards on 344 rushes and had two five-TD games and four four-TD games. He nearly made third and fourth downs unnecessary.

1988 Season Statistics:

Rush: 344   Yds: 2,628   TD: 39
Runners-Up: 2. Rodney Peete,
Southern California
3. Troy Aikman, UCLA
4. Steve Walsh, Miami
5. Major Harris, West Virginia

1989 Andre Ware,
Houston Quarterback

As a fan and/or student of college football, you well know that the University of Houston has seldom been regarded as a prowess in college football. Shoot, even the waitresses at all the Southwestern Conference truck-stop restaurants can testify to that, even under oath.

But exceptions do spring up. At the conclusion of the '88 season, Houston appeared in 18th place in the final national rankings, right there between perennial powers Alabama and LSU. The following season, Houston moved up to 14th place, just below Arkansas but directly ahead of Penn State, Michigan State and Pittsburgh.

Coaching is always featured as a major cause for a dramatic turnaround in a program's success. But an even more significant reason is the player who responds superbly to the program's demands. Andre Ware delivered well for Houston in '88, mastering Jack Pardee's run-and-shoot offense and racking up awesome stats: 2,507 passing yards and 26 TD passes. The next year was historical. Ware threw 578 passes, a previously unheard-of 52 per game, and completed 365 of those despite playing just a little more than the first half of most games. He led the Cougars to a 9-2 season record and relied on newspapers to trumpet his accomplishments due to the fact that Houston was not scheduled for any national television appearances in '89.

Stats won Ware the Heisman in '89. He set 26 NCAA and 15 Southwest Conference records that season, averaging over 427 passing yards and over four TD passes for 11 games. A consensus All American, Ware was drafted by the Detroit Lions after his junior year.

1989 Season Statistics:

Att/Comp: 578/365   Yds: 4,699   TD: 46
Runners-Up: 2. Anthony Thompson, Indiana
3. Major Harris, West Virginia
4. Tony Rice, Notre Dame
5. Darian Hagan, Colorado

1990

Ty Detmer,
Brigham Young Quarterback

For ten years, the voters of the Heisman started paying more than a little attention to players from the Western Athletic Conference, particularly quarterbacks from Brigham Young University. In '81, QB Jim McMahon finished third in Heisman voting and in '83 Steve Young also finished third. In '90 yet another BYU QB came along and won the whole enchilada. It was not a fluke. No signal caller in the history of the game had a season to match Ty Detmer's '90 season.

numbers sent analysts running to the record books. Ty's 5,199 aerial yards eclipsed the old mark by more than 400 yards, and he went on to break 41 other NCAA records. And he accomplished all this in only his junior year!

Ty's extraordinary exploits did not go unnoticed. Among the 25 major awards he won in '90, the most notable were the Heisman and seven first team All American selections. By the time he graduated in '92, he owned 59 NCAA records, including an incredible 121 TD passes.

Ty first started to gain national recognition in the '89 season, his sophomore season at BYU. He passed for an astronomical 4,560 yards and led the Cougars to the WAC championship. He put the cap on this breakout season by throwing for an NCAA bowl record 576 yards in the Holiday Bowl against Penn State.

Going into the '90 season, many people wondered what Ty could possibly do to top his sophomore year. All Ty did was have the best season a quarterback ever had in the annals of college football. The young man's poise and uncanny accuracy brought comparisons to none other than Joe Montana, and his awe-inspiring

1990 Season Statistics:

Att/Comp: 562/361   Yds: 5,188   TD: 41
Runners-Up: 2. Raghib Ismail, Notre Dame
3. Eric Bieniemy, Colorado
4. Shawn Moore, Virginia
5. David Klingler, Houston
6. Herman Moore, Virginia
7. Greg Lewis, Washington
8. Craig Erickson, Miami
9. Darren Lewis, Texas A&M
10. Mike Mayweather, Army

1991

Desmond Howard,
Michigan Wide Receiver

In '88, Desmond Howard was one of thousands of Heisman hopefuls newly arrived on a college campus just trying to figure things out and find a fit for himself. That year, like so many others, Desmond spent time on the pine. He didn't get into a single game.

The next year, Desmond got enough game time to be recognized by The Sporting News as one of the nation's outstanding receivers. He was a backup flanker and the leading kickoff returner on the team. He returned two kickoffs for 62 yards against Notre Dame.

In '90, Desmond stepped up. He racked up 504 yards on kickoff returns and another 1,025 receiving on 63 receptions. The nation's coaches gave him honorable mention on their All America teams and the media selected him first-team All Big 10.

At the beginning of the '91 season, there were no shoo-ins for the Heisman. A big play at the right time would help anybody's chances. How 'bout the Notre Dame-Michigan game, on national television, with the Wolverines trying to end a string of four straight losses to the Irish?

On a crucial fourth-down-and-inches play that

decided the outcome, Desmond broke into the end zone. His high school teammate, Elvis Grbac, launched a floating spiral that seemed too high to be caught. But Desmond got under it, leaped high and cradled the ball in outstretched hands. Dozens of cameras caught it, too. The Catch, of all the catches in Michigan football history, was now official. Now, to win the Heisman, all Howard had to do was make dazzling receptions and run back kicks with reckless abandon for the rest of the season, which he did indeed do.

1991 Season Statistics:

Rec: 61   Yds: 950   TD: 23

Runners-Up: 2. Casey Weldon, Florida State
3. Ty Detmer, Brigham Young
4. Steve Emtman, Washington
5. Shane Matthews, Florida
6. Vaughn Dunbar, Indiana
7. Jeff Blake, East Carolina
8. Terrell Buckley, Florida State
9. Marshall Faulk,
    San Diego State
10. Bucky Richardson, Texas A&M

1992 Gino Torretta,
Miami (FL) Quarterback

Gino Torretta was the other fifth-year senior at Miami who used his time in waiting to superior advantage. When he finally got his chance to lead, all Torretta did was take the Hurricanes to the national championship in '91 with a perfect record of 12-0 and to an 11-1 season in '92.

A 6-foot, 205 pounder from Pinole Valley, California, Torretta turned down offers to play at Washington, Washington State, Stanford and California to continue the fabled QB parade at Miami. Torretta sported a 26-2 record as the Hurricanes' starting quarterback, including a 3-1 record as a redshirt freshman in UM's '89 national championship season.

Torretta became the most celebrated player in Miami history. In addition to winning the Heisman, he also was on everyone's All America team, won the Maxwell Trophy and the Davey O'Brien Award and a whole bunch of others. By the time he left Miami, he claimed 11 records on Miami's career and single-game lists, including a couple of astounding ones:

555 completions and 123 pass attempts without an interception.

Torretta had the good fortune to be featured on national television and he also had the talent and pluck to profit from it. In a showdown matchup against San Diego State and Heisman hopeful Marshall Faulk, Torretta threw for four touchdowns.

Against arch rival Florida State and another Heisman hopeful (Marvin Jones, who finished fourth in '92), he mounted a comeback drive by running for 14 yards and a first down on a third-and-12 play, then hit Lamar Thomas for a 33-yard winning TD with 6:50 left to play.

1992 Season Statistics:
Att/Comp: 402/228   Yds: 3,060   TD: 19
Runners-Up: 2. Marshall Faulk,
San Diego State
3. Garrison Hearst, Georgia
4. Marvin Jones, Florida State
5. Reggie Brooks, Notre Dame

1993 Charlie Ward,
Florida State Quarterback

One sure way to get recognized by Heisman voters is to be the All American quarterback of a team that goes 23-2 over two seasons and ends up second and first in the country, which is what quarterback Charlie Ward did for the Florida State Seminoles in '92 and '93.

The Florida State media guide claims Ward as "the most heralded athlete in the history of college football." The praise would be high enough if it proclaimed him to be only the most heralded of the dozens of All American Seminoles who've put FSU at the very top of college football. In '99, Florida State finished unbeaten at No. 1 again and enjoyed its 13th straight year among the nation's Top 4.

In the 66 seasons of the Heisman, Ward is the only Seminole to win the Heisman. The focus was surely on him in '93. From season's beginning, he was the Heisman frontrunner. With pressure on him every week, he responded not only with consistently high performances on the field, but also with the kind of inspired leadership and social behavior it takes when

one is that much in the spotlight.

Ward was nimble for a man his size. At 6-2 and 190, he had a commanding view of defenses from the shotgun and had phenomenal escape skills. He averaged six yards every time he had to carry the ball. But it was as a passer that he ruined defenses. His completion average was close to 70% and he could throw long as well as short.

It was in one of his two defeats that Ward showed his mettle. In the heart-stopping loss to Notre Dame in South Bend, he still got 300 yards passing and came within a whisker of saving the day for the Seminoles.

1993 Season Statistics:
Att/Comp: 380/264   Yds: 3,032   TD: 27
Runners-Up: 2. Heath Shuler, Tennessee
3. David Palmer, Alabama
4. Marshall Faulk, San Diego State
5. Glenn Foley, Boston College

1994 Rashaan Salaam,
Colorado Running Back

Rashaan Salaam possessed all the ingredients required to become a Heisman winner. First, he had the genes. His dad played freshman football at Colorado before transferring to San Diego State, then going to the Cincinnati Bengals and then Canadian pro ball. An uncle played free safety at Utah State and a cousin was a wide receiver at Fresno State.

Salaam grew up in a tough neighborhood, in the predominately black Skyline neighborhood of San Diego. When he encountered problems, his mother enrolled him in the posh La Jolla Country Day School at a cost of $8,000 a year. There he flourished. With good size (6-1 and 215) to go with 4.4 40-second speed, he wreaked havoc among the preppies. In his first varsity game, at age 15, he rolled to 368 yards and five touchdowns. He made every high school All America team and was named MVP of the annual San Diego County All Star game.

When Salaam got to Colorado, it was same-old, same-old. He was just the fourth running back in Division 1-A history to break the magic 2,000-yard barrier. In the '94 season he gained 100 yards in 10 games and 200 yards four times against Big Eight

competition, averaging 186.8 yards per game – fourth best in NCAA history. And he accomplished all this by playing in only six fourth quarters during his team's 11-1 season.

For the season, he led the NCAA in rushing, scoring and all-purpose yards (213.5 per game) and was the major factor in Colorado's ranking of third in the nation.

After winning the Heisman, Salaam became the youngest player ever drafted by the pros. He was a first-round choice of the Chicago Bears.

1994 Season Statistics:

Rush: 298   Yds: 2,055   TD: 24

Runners-Up: 2. Ki-Jana Carter, Penn State
3. Steve McNair, Alcorn State
4. Kerry Collins, Penn State
5. Jay Barker, Alabama
6. Warren Sapp, Miami
7. Eric Zeier, Georgia
8. Lawrence Phillips, Nebraska
9. Napoleon Kaufman, Washington
10. Zach Wiegert, Nebraska

1995 Eddie George,
Ohio State Running Back

Watch out, Fighting Irish; the Buckeyes are gaining on you.

When the '95 football season started, Notre Dame had seven Heisman winners to Ohio State's five. And both teams had nobody but longshot contenders for the '95 award.

As the season progressed, a fellow named George went from longshot to runaway. In becoming Ohio State's sixth Heisman winner, Eddie George etched his name into OSU records books by rushing for 1,927 yards and 24 touchdowns. Included in that yardage were three 200-plus-yard games, one of which was an Ohio State record 314 yards against Illinois. The 6-3, 227-pound George wound up the '95 season leading the country in scoring with an average of 12.1 points per game.

A native of Philadelphia, George averaged 5.9 yards on 328 carries. He also set a school receiving record for a running back with 47 catches.

Ironically, it was against Notre Dame when the national press started equating George to the Heisman. Two weeks earlier, he had rushed for 219

yards in an OSU thumping of Washington and in the fourth game of the season he proved he was no fluke against Notre Dame. In this one, he gained 207 yards in leading the Buckeyes to a big 45-26 win.

George helped keep the Buckeyes ranked at the top of the polls most of the '95 season. They didn't lose until the final game of the regular season when rival Michigan caught them in Ann Arbor, 31-23. The Buckeyes then lost to Tennessee in the Citrus Bowl, 20-14.

George was a first-round NFL draft choice and was the '96 NFL Rookie of the Year. He also started and starred in the 2000 Super Bowl.

1995 Season Statistics:

Rush: 328   Yds: 1,927   TD: 24

Runners-Up: 2. *Tommy Frazier, Nebraska*
3. *Danny Wuerffel, Florida*
4. *Darnell Autry, Northwestern*
5. *Troy Davis, Iowa State*

1996 Danny Wuerffel,
Florida Quarterback

Over the recent years, there's been something historic about playing QB at Florida. Steve Spurrier, the current coach, started it by winning the Heisman back in '66. Five years later, John Reaves completed his Florida career as college football's all-time passing leader. Then in '87, walk-on Kerwin Bell set the SEC's all-time record for TD passes and passing yards. That was broken five years later by Shane Matthews. Then along came Danny Wuerffel to break everybody's records.

Wuerffel was a first-team All American in '95 and '96 and a two-time recipient of the Davey O'Brien National QB of the Year Award. In his career he completed 708 of 1,170 passes for 10,875 yards, which was fifth best in major college history. He also connected on 114 TD passes, best in SEC history and second best for major colleges.

Wuerffel was the NCAA's best in history in pass-efficiency with a rating of 163.56 and in percentage of passes for touchdowns (9.74).

Wuerffel's TD-passes-per-season were: 22, 18, 35 and 39. Even more impressive were Florida's record the four years with Wuerffel at quarterback: 11-2 in '93, 10-2-1 in '94, 12-1 in '95 and 12-1 in '96. The Gators were SEC champs each of those four years.

To put a perfect ending to an outstanding career, Wuerffel led the Gators to the national championship in his senior season. Florida finished the regular season with an 11-1 record, losing only to arch rival Florida State by a field goal, 24-21, in Tallahassee in a match between Nos. 1 and 2. Florida then won the Sugar Bowl rematch for No. 1 by swamping the Seminoles by a score of 52-20.

1935 Season Statistics:
Att/Comp: 360/207   Yds: 3,625   TD: 39
Runners-Up: 2. Troy Davis, Iowa State
3. Jake Plummer, Arizona State
4. Orlando Pace, Ohio State
5. Warrick Dunn, Florida State

1997

Charles Woodson,
Michigan Cornerback

In Charles Woodson's never-to-be-forgotten '97 season, he did about everything but tape ankles. When it came time to pick the All America teams, some experts didn't know where to place him. Woodson had an outstanding season at cornerback, receiver and punt returner.

Woodson won the Jim Thorpe Award, given to the best defensive player of the year. The Davey O'Brien Quarterback Award and the Maxwell Award went to Peyton Manning of Tennessee. Then, in one of the closest and most debated Heisman votes in history, Woodson edged Manning to win college football's most cherished trophy.

Woodson made plays of spectacular variety in '97. Against Colorado, he set up Michigan's first 10 points with an interception and a 29-yard pass reception. He scored the winning touchdown on a reception against Baylor. He had an interception and a reception in the Indiana game. Against Northwestern, he had five tackles, a sack, a reception and an interception ... two interceptions at Michigan State ...

ran once against Minnesota, for a 33-yard touchdown and also returned three punts and caught a pass ... got two tackles, two third-down pass breakups and a 37-yard TD pass against Penn State ... got 137 all-purpose yards against Ohio State, including a 78-yard punt return for a touchdown.

Woodson and the Wolverines finished the '97 season with a 21-6 victory over Washington State in the Rose Bowl to go 12-0 on the season and to claim a share of the national championship with Nebraska. Woodson was then drafted fourth overall by the Oakland Raiders. He was named the NFL Defensive Rookie of the Year in '98.

1997 Season Statistics:

7 interceptions   Rec: 11   Yds: 231   TD: 4
Runners-Up: 2. Peyton Manning, Tennessee
3. Ryan Leaf, Washington State
4. Randy Moss, Marshall
5. Ricky Williams, Texas

1998 Ricky Williams,
Texas Tailback

In January of '98, Ricky Williams was the star of a press conference in Austin, Texas. He was there to announce he would return to Texas for his senior season and was asked how many yards he needed to pass Tony Dorsett's all-time NCAA major college rushing record.

Ricky's reply was, "something like 1,928." That's what it would take to not only beat the record but to also win the Heisman. Piece of cake.

He finished the '97 season with 1,893 yards. He would be the featured Longhorn back again in '98, but he would also be a marked man. He could expect eight- and nine-man fronts and they'd all be keying on him.

After the third game of the season, chances of his winning the Heisman looked grim. Kansas State trounced Texas and held Williams to 43 yards on 25 carries. There was doubt that he was still in the race.

Williams bounced back from a 48-7 loss to Kansas State by racking up 318 yards and six touchdowns in a 59-21 shellacking of Rice. The following week, he shredded the Iowa State defense for 350 yards and five touchdowns and suddenly he was not just a Heisman candidate, he was the clear frontrunner.

He got 139 yards against Oklahoma, then 259 in

the Baylor game and 150 on 37 carries against the vaunted Nebraska Blackshirt defense. With three games left, he needed 294 yards to pass Dorsett. Against Oklahoma State, he gained only 90. He got 141 against Texas Tech. One more game, a final chance to win the Heisman. Williams against Texas A&M's defense, No. 2 in the country. Final score: Texas 26, Texas A&M 24. Williams ran 44 times for 259 yards, breaking Dorsett's record and winning the Heisman in one of the most thrilling finishes in history.

1998 Season Statistics:

Rush: 361 Yards: 2,124 TD: 28
Runners-Up: 2. Michael Bishop, Kansas State
3. **Cade NcNown, UCLA**
4. **Tim Couch, Kentucky**
5. **Donovan McNabb, Syracuse**
5. **Duante Culpepper,**
   Central Florida
6. **Champ Bailey, Georgia**
7. **Torry Holt, North Carolina State**
8. **Joe Germaine, Ohio State**
9. **Shaun King, Tulane**

1999 Ron Dayne,
Wisconsin Running Back

If the nickname "The Horse" hadn't been already taken by a previous Wisconsin Heisman winner (Alan Ameche in '54), it surely would have fit the recipient of the '99 Heisman. Instead, Ron Dayne had to settle for this: "The Great Dayne."

Doggy nickname aside, Dayne's numbers at Wisconsin overwhelmed the '99 Heisman voters and he won by one of the biggest margins ever, with 2,042 points to 994 for Joe Hamilton of Georgia Tech.

Ron Dayne had more than a great college career. He had the best ever by a running back. He set the all-time career rushing record with 6,397 yards. That's over three and a half miles, folks!

Dayne's numbers were mind boggling. Nobody ever had more to work with than the Wisconsin sports info dispensers. In his four 1,000-plus seasons, he averaged 148.8 yards a game. He personally outrushed the opposing team 28 times in 42 starts. He averaged 114.9 yards rushing vs. nationally ranked teams (14). He only lost nine fumbles in 1,186 carries (0.75%). He had 183 career runs of at least 10 yards against defenses geared to slow him with up to nine players

"in the box."

The trophies he won were numerous. Think of what he qualified for and he won it. Another accolade, this one from CNN/SI analyst Trev Alberts: "I like this guy more all the time. He's never had a quarterback who could pass more than 20 yards and everyone knows he will run."

Dayne's coach, Barry Alvarez: "Ron really exemplifies our program – blue collar, tough, hard-nosed." It will be interesting to see how good the Wisconsin program will be without Dayne.

1999 Season Statistics:

Rush: 303   Yds: 1,834   TD: 19

Runners-Up:
2. Joe Hamilton, Georgia Tech
3. Michael Vick, Virginia Tech
4. Drew Brees, Purdue
5. Chad Pennington, Marshall
6. Peter Warrick, Florida State
8. Thomas Jones, Virginia
9. LaVar Arrington, Penn State
10. Tim Rattay, Louisiana Tech

Does winning the Heisman mean that the recipient will have a fantastic pro career and be considered one of the greatest players of all time?

Not necessarily.

The Sports Illustrated Jinx?

**Not one of the first 11
on Sports Illustrated's list of
The Greatest Players of All Time
won the Heisman.**

1. Jim Brown
2. Jerry Rice
3. Joe Montana
4. Lawrence Taylor
5. Johnny Unitas
6. Don Hutson
7. Otto Graham
8. Walter Payton
9. Dick Butkus
10. Bob Lilly
11. Sammy Baugh

**And only one
made the Second Team**

**12. Barry Sanders won the
Heisman in 1988.**

13. Deacon Jones

14. Joe Greene

15. Gino Marchetti

16. John Elway

17. Anthony Munoz

18. Ray Nitschke

19. Night Train Lane

20. John Hannah

21. Gale Sayers

22. Reggie White

Heisman Trivia

1. Name the player who succeeded the great Slingin' Sammy Baugh in college.

2. Name the three schools that produced back-to-back Heisman winners.

3. Which college holds the alltime record for wins?

4. In a classic upset of Notre Dame, this player scored all the points for his team and punted 16 times, the last one a game-winner to the Irish five-yard line. Who was he?

5. Name the first Heisman winner to be chosen first in the NFL draft.

6. Name the Heisman winner they called Flatfoot Frankie.

7. Who was the player who missed the final four games of the season the year he won the Heisman?

8. Name the two linemen who won the Heisman.

9. Name the first of the three Oklahoma halfbacks who won the Heisman.

10. Which Heisman winner played in the Final Four?

Answers to Heisman Trivia

1. Davey O'Brien, TCU halfback. 1938 Heisman winner.

2. One was Yale. End Larry Kelley won the Heisman in '36 and Clint Frank won it in '37. Another was Army. Doc Blanchard won the Heisman in '45 when backfield-mate Glenn Davis was second. Davis won it in '46 and Blanchard finished fourth. And Ohio State running back Archie Griffin won the Heisman in '74. The next year's winner was the same man, same school. Griffin came close in '73, when three Buckeyes finished in the top six. Second was tackle John Hicks, Griffin was fifth and linebacker Randy Gradishar was sixth.

3. Yale.

4. Nile Kinnick, Iowa halfback. The '39 Heisman winner.

5. Jay Berwanger, University of Chicago halfback. Other number-one NFL picks included '56 Heisman winner Paul Hornung, a bonus pick by the Green Bay Packers. Ernie Davis, '61 Heisman winner, was the No. 1 pick in the '62 NFL draft. Davis was selected by the Cleveland Browns, who intended to pair him with Jim Brown.

6. Frank Sinkwich, Georgia halfback. The '42 Heisman winner.

7. Angelo Bertelli, Notre Dame quarterback. The '43 Heisman winner. With four games left that season, Bertelli left South Bend, Indiana and reported for U.S. Marine training at Parris Island, South Carolina.

8. Larry Kelley, Yale end. The '36 Heisman winner. And Leon Hart, Notre Dame end. The '49 Heisman winner.

9. Billy Vessels, Oklahoma halfback. The '52 Heisman winner.

10. Terry Baker, Oregon State quarterback. The '62 Heisman winner.

Heisman Watch 2000

Anything can happen and no doubt will. That's what makes Heisman watching interesting as each season progresses. Records, made to be broken, will indeed be broken. Somebody will have a great game on national television in this season's game of the century. Favorites will falter and unheard-ofs will rise from nowhere to national prominence and with the help of hype from a biased sports information director will get on the Heisman list. But based on what happened last year and is forecast this year, these are the front-runners – at least until the second or third game of the season.

1. **Michael Vick,** Virginia Tech quarterback, was a redshirt freshman in 1999, but anybody who saw him play – especially against Florida State in the Sugar Bowl – knows he has to be the Heisman frontrunner going into the 2000 season. Vick led his Hokies to an 11-1 season last year, winning the respect of all who watched him. His main critic, his coach, Frank Beamer, had this to say about Vicks: "He plays the game better than anybody I've ever seen. He just does it. He can run so fast. He can throw so well. He makes something out of nothing. And he's a great guy. You see him smile, and you want to smile back at him." Vick finished third in the 1999 Heisman voting and the two players ahead of him have both been graduated.

Michael Vick

Drew Brees

2. **Drew Brees** has had three seasons to make a name for himself at Purdue and the gifted quarterback has made the most of them. A fourth-place finisher in the '99 Heisman balloting, Brees will be entering his third season as the Boilermaker starter and if he stays on the track he's been on, he'll leave school with nearly every Big Ten passing mark. The irony of the Brees situation is, though he's likely to become the most prolific Big Ten passer of all time, Heisman voters may require a conference championship to put Brees on top. If his Boilermakers finish ahead of Wisconsin, Michigan, Illinois, Penn State, Ohio State and Michigan State, the Heisman should be his.

3. **Quincy Carter** of Georgia is currently the third-ranked quarterback in the nation for the upcoming season. But he plays for a powerful team and has a terrific receiving corps. And he has two good years behind him. But where it will really matter is when he leads the his mates out onto the Georgia turf to take on Tennessee and down in

Quincy Carter

Jacksonville to do battle with Florida. Two wins here would certainly tighten the field.

4. **Eric Crouch** is the very gifted quarterback of the preseason favorites to win the national championship. Many believe that he is the best QB to ever play at Nebraska. But Nebraska is so deep and talented, Eric Crouch will be sharing headlines with other Cornhuskers this season. To rise above Vick and Brees will take some doing.

5. **Chris Weinke** is the quarterback for the defending national champions, Florida State. But Weinke's most prolific receivers from last year are now in the NFL and early Seminole scouting reports indicate that FSU will rely more on the ground than the air this year.

6. **Freddie Milons,** WR Alabama. He's versatile, along the lines of Desmond Howard, Michigan's 1991 Heisman winner. He's a great receiver, an exciting runner and talented enough to play quarterback. Plus, he might be the best return man in the country.

7. **Kurt Kittner** will be gunning for the Big Ten championship, the national championship and the Heisman. Coming close to attaining any of those three goals will require 12 outstanding performances for this Illinois junior QB. But Kittner, who has mastered coach Ron Turner's sophisticated pro-style offense, appears up for the challenge. So do the rest of the Illini. Twelve starters and 41 lettermen return from a team that went 8-4 last season and produced the most points in school history.

8. **LaDainian Tomlinson** is a name to remember. Player, too. Against UTEP last year, the TCU halfback rushed for 406 yards. He didn't fare as well against tougher competition, but still racked up 1,850 yards. If he gets 2,000 this season and if TCU, as expected, has a great season, Tomlinson will get Heisman votes.

9. **Marques Tuiasosopo** may cause the eastern sportswriters to sharpen their spelling abilities before this season's over. Tuiasosopo is already well known in the west. The 215-pound Washington quarterback is considered the key offensive player in the Pac 10. That conference is staging a comeback to lofty status and with Tuiasosopo running the Husky option and throwing to receiver Chris Juergens and pro prospect TE Jerramy Stevens, Tuiasosopo could well end up at the DAC Heisman Room waiting for his name to be called and properly pronounced.

10. **Jared Lorenzen and Dusty Bonner.** Lorenzen is the redshirt freshman who was supposed to ride the Kentucky bench this season and watch junior QB Dusty Bonner again lead the SEC in every passing category (last year Bonner threw 468 times and hit on 65 percent of his attempts). Then something happened after this year's spring practice. Coach Hal Mumme sat down and studied film for a few days. When he emerged, he announced that he was demoting Bonner and replacing him with Lorenzen. Mumme thought Lorenzen had the better arm. Bonner abruptly transferred. If you have any compassion for coach Mumme, keep your fingers crossed as you keep your eyes on both Bonner and Lorenzen.

Heisman Memorial Trophy Winners

Ron Dayne, University of Wisconsin running back and 1999 Heisman winner.

Year	Name	School	Position	Coach	Team's Nat'l Rank
1999	Ron Dayne	Wisconsin	Tailback	Barry Alvarez	4th
1998	Ricky Williams	Texas	Tailback	Mack Brown	15th
1997	Charles Woodson	Michigan	DB/WR	Lloyd Carr	1st
1996	Danny Wuerffel	Florida	QB	Steve Spurrier	1st
1995	Eddie George	Ohio State	RB	John Cooper	6th
1994	Rashaan Salaam	Colorado	RB	Bill McCartney	3rd
1993	Charlie Ward	Florida State	QB	Bobby Bowden	1st
1992	Gino Torretta	Miami	QB	Dennis Erickson	3rd
1991	Desmond Howard	Michigan	WR	Gary Moeller	6th
1990	Ty Dettmer	Brigham Young	QB	LaVell Edwards	22nd
1989	Andre Ware	Houston	QB	Jack Pardee	14th
1988	Barry Sanders	Oklahoma State	RB	Pat Jones	11th
1987	Tim Brown	Notre Dame	WR	Lou Holtz	17th
1986	Vinny Testaverde	Miami	QB	Jimmy Johnson	2nd
1985	Bo Jackson	Auburn	RB	Pat Dye	Not Ranked
1984	Doug Flutie	Boston College	QB	Jack Bicknell	5th
1983	Mike Rozier	Nebraska	RB	Tom Osborne	2nd
1982	Herschel Walker	Georgia	RB	Vince Dooley	4th
1981	Marcus Allen	Southern Cal	RB	John Robinson	14th
1980	George Rogers	South Carolina	RB	Jim Carlen	Not Ranked
1979	Charles White	Southern Cal	RB	John Robinson	2nd
1978	Billy Sims	Oklahoma	RB	Barry Switzer	3rd
1977	Earl Campbell	Texas	RB	Fred Akers	4th
1976	Tony Dorsett	Pittsburgh	RB	Johnny Majors	1st
1975	Archie Griffin	Ohio State	RB	Woody Hayes	4th
1974	Archie Griffin	Ohio State	RB	Woody Hayes	4th
1973	John Cappelletti	Penn State	RB	Joe Paterno	5th
1972	Johnny Rodgers	Nebraska	WR	Bob Devaney	4th
1971	Pat Sullivan	Auburn	QB	Shug Jordan	12th
1970	Jim Plunkett	Stanford	QB	John Ralston	8th
1969	Steve Owens	Oklahoma	RB	Chuck Fairbanks	Not Ranked
1968	O.J. Simpson	Southern Cal	RB	John McKay	4th
1967	Gary Beban	UCLA	QB	Tommy Prothro	11th

Heisman Memorial Trophy Winners (continued)

Year	Name	School	Position	Coach	Team's Nat'l Rank
1966	Steve Spurrier	Florida	QB	Ray Graves	11th
1965	Mike Garrett	Southern Cal	RB	John McKay	10th
1964	John Huarte	Notre Dame	QB	Ara Parseghian	3rd
1963	Roger Staubach	Navy	QB	Wayne Hardin	2nd
1962	Terry Baker	Oregon State	QB	Tommy Prothro	16th
1961	Ernie Davis	Syracuse	RB	Ben Schwartzwalder	14th
1960	Joe Bellino	Navy	RB	Wayne Hardin	4th
1959	Billy Cannon	LSU	RB	Paul Dietzel	3rd
1958	Pete Dawkins	Army	RB	Red Blaik	3rd
1957	John David Crow	Texas A&M	RB	Bear Bryant	9th
1956	Paul Hornung	Notre Dame	QB	Terry Brennan	Not Ranked
1955	Howard Cassady	Ohio State	HB	Woody Hayes	5th
1954	Alan Ameche	Wisconsin	FB	Ivy Williamson	9th
1953	Johnny Lattner	Notre Dame	QB	Frank Leahy	2nd
1952	Billy Vessels	Oklahoma	HB	Bud Wilkinson	4th
1951	Dick Kazmaier	Princeton	HB	Charlie Caldwell	6th
1950	Vic Janowicz	Ohio State	HB	Wes Fesler	14th
1949	Leon Hart	Notre Dame	E	Frank Leahy	1st
1948	Doak Walker	SMU	HB	Matty Bell	10th
1947	Johnny Lujack	Notre Dame	QB	Frank Leahy	1st
1946	Glenn Davis	Army	HB	Red Blaik	2nd
1945	Doc Blanchard	Army	FB	Red Blaik	1st
1944	Les Horvath	Ohio State	QB/HB	Carroll Widdoes	2nd
1943	Angelo Bertelli	Notre Dame	QB	Ed McKeever	1st
1942	Frank Sinkwich	Georgia	HB	Wally Butts	2nd
1941	Bruce Smith	Minnesota	HB	Bernie Bierman	1st
1940	Tom Harmon	Michigan	HB	Fritz Crisler	3rd
1939	Nile Kinnick	Iowa	HB	Eddie Anderson	9th
1938	Davey O'Brien	Texas Christian	HB	Dutch Meyer	1st
1937	Clint Frank	Yale	HB	Ducky Pond	12th
1936	Larry Kelley	Yale	E	Ducky Pond	12th
1935	Jay Berwanger	Chicago	HB	Clark Shaughnessy	Not Ranked

ABOUT THE AUTHOR

After playing football and honing writing skills by writing sports for five years in California, Don Gwaltney moved to Chicago and spent 35 years creating ad campaigns. He wrote the first 50 ads for Marlboro Country, acclaimed the most successful ad/marketing campaign of the 20th century. He authored the much-parodied This is Not Your Father's Oldsmobile campaign. The song for that was voted best ad song for the year in the world in 1991. He began writing books in 1995. Among them are a novel, <u>The Bandit Joaquin</u>; a recollection of folks met along the way, <u>Characters, Legends and $3 Bills</u>; a coffeetable masterpiece, <u>The Not to be Forgotten Forties</u>; a red meat lover's bible, <u>The Steak Lover's Handbook</u>; and recently, another cookbook, <u>The Best Pizza Recipes in America.</u> Don currently lives on Spring Island in South Carolina with his wife, Carol.